Northwestern University
STUDIES IN *Phenomenology &*
Existential Philosophy

The Problem of God

Henry Duméry

Translated, with an Introduction by

A critical examination of the category of

The Absolute and the scheme of transcendence

The Problem of God

in Philosophy of Religion

CHARLES COURTNEY

NORTHWESTERN UNIVERSITY PRESS

1 9 6 4

4/1965
Chi.

To Paul Ricoeur

TRANSLATOR'S

Note

FOR THE CONVENIENCE of the reader, in each case where there exists an English translation of a work referred to by Duméry, I have provided a reference to the translation. But since I have translated the French text throughout, the English version here does not necessarily agree with the translation cited. All references and comments that I have added are placed within brackets.

I am grateful to several persons for their generous assistance. Several long discussions with Henry Duméry greatly increased my comprehension of his book. Professors James M. Edie and John Wild and Messrs. David Carr and Charles Kelbley read and criticized parts of an early draft of the translation. I wish to express special thanks to Professor Samuel M. Thompson who read the entire manuscript and made several important suggestions. If the text is in readable English, much of the credit should go to my wife Bonnie who, after reading fairy tales to Robin, devoted several long evenings to reading the manuscript to me. I am wholly responsible, of course, for the defects that remain.   C. C.

Contents

Introduction

The Problem of God [1] is part of one of the most important philosophies of religion written in recent times. The author, Henry Duméry, a French philosopher born in 1920, is Professor in the University of Caen and Administrative Secretary of the International Institute of Philosophy in Paris.

Duméry seeks to develop a position that respects the concrete data of religion and also recognizes the unlimited scope of philosophical criticism. Thus philosophy of religion is not religion stated philosophically; the preposition "of" is not used possessively. Philosophy of religion is an autonomous reflective discipline which is, in principle, applicable to all religious phenomena. Duméry deals exclusively with the Biblical religions because he knows them best; this fact, however, is accidental to his intention of developing a universally valid philosophy of religion.

---

1. *Le problème de Dieu en philosophie de la religion: examen critique de la catégorie d'Absolu et du schème de transcendance* (Paris, 1957).

The contrast between this approach and other widely accepted notions of philosophy of religion is evident. At the same time his work is distinguished by the richness and variety of its historical associations. Probably Duméry's closest alignment is with phenomenology; but this alignment is neither uncritical nor exclusive. His first philosophical works were competent, fresh, and sympathetic expositions of the philosophy of Maurice Blondel.[2] The erudition and sureness of interpretation that mark all his books reveal his firm command of Western philosophy. The most significant result of his historical appreciations, a brilliant restatement and development of negative theology, is found in this volume. Gabriel Widmer maintains that Duméry has given the question of the relationship between faith and criticism a scope that it has not had since the end of the seventeenth century.[3]

It is important to realize the chronological and systematic place of *The Problem of God* in Duméry's thought. It was written during the first years of his affiliation (1950–57) with the French National Center for Scientific Research (C.N.R.S.). It was complemented and corrected, especially with respect to the doctrine of analogy and its relationships to henology and ontology, by *La foi n'est pas un cri,* followed by *Foi et institution.*[4]

2. *La Philosophie de l'action: essai sur l'intellectualisme blondélien* (Paris, 1948); *Blondel et la religion: essai critique sur la "Lettre" de 1896* (Paris, 1954). Duméry's most recent book is *Raison et religion dans la philosophie de l'action* (Paris, 1963).

3. Gabriel Widmer, "Synthèse chrétienne et exigence critique: la philosophie de la religion selon Henry Duméry," *Revue de théologie et de philosophie,* 3rd series, VIII (1958), p. 217.

4. Paris, 1959. It is on the condition that the reader take account of these corrections that the author has authorized the publication of the present translation.

In a work yet to appear, entitled *Le sens de l'absolu en philosophie de la religion,* the problem treated here will be taken up in a manner more specifically phenomenological. It will study "the constitution of the meaning of the Absolute, the constituting meaning of the Absolute, and the relationships between the constituting meaning and the constituted meanings." [5]

The Problem of God was written during the same period as the works which Duméry presented to the Sorbonne for the Doctorat d'État.[6] As the Preface indicates, they are systematically related. Duméry's method and doctrine were developed simultaneously and are not separable. *Philosophie de la reliqion* is the sequel of *Critique et religion* and "can be understood only as the prolongation of our methodological inquiry." [7] An ensemble of twelve doctrinal studies is announced; the present volume is the first of these, and the categories of the subject, grace, and faith are treated in the two volumes of *Philosophie de la religion.*[8]

Among the doctrinal studies, those concerning the Absolute and the subject have a special place. Together they form a prolegomenon to all other philosophical inquiry. These treatises could be called first philosophy; the principles they establish are metaphysical. Duméry says that the study of the nature of the human subject

5. Personal communication from the author, June 11, 1963.

6. The complementary thesis was *Critique et religion: problèmes de méthode en philosophie de la religion* (Paris, 1957). The principal thesis was *Philosophie de la religion: essai sur la signification du christianisme,* I–II (Paris, 1957). These books plus *La foi n'est pas un cri* (1st ed., Paris, 1957) and *Le problème de Dieu* have encountered official resistance in the Roman Catholic Church.

7. *Philosophie de la religion,* I, p. v.

8. Other categories to be studied are the contingent, miracle, the Word, the universal, sin, and love. Cf. *Ibid.,* p. vii.

"will consist in systematically disclosing the presuppositions of all critical interpretation of the activities of the human subject." [9] Conversely, the full elaboration of any specific instance of philosophical reflection entails an examination of these two categories. With respect to the philosophy of religion, Duméry says, "once informed of the critical value of the idea of the Absolute and of the nature and exigencies of human subjectivity, we will have in hand the two terms of the religious relationship. . . ." [10] Moreover, "to study religion without examining the meaning, validity, and scope of the categories of the Absolute and the subject . . . is literally to destroy it." [11]

The preceding paragraphs indicate how comprehensive and well ordered Duméry's philosophy is. But it is not necessary to know the entire corpus to understand *The Problem of God*. The reason is that he develops his own position by way of constant dialectical conversation with other well-known approaches. The three most important examples of this can be illustrated briefly. In Chapter One he attempts to show that an objectivist approach to the problem of God (apparently he is thinking of certain versions of Thomism) is insufficient because it is not radically critical of the concepts of cause and determination. Later, in Section III of Chapter Two, he suggests that Thomism at its best, especially in St. Thomas, actually employs principles similar to his own. Léon Brunschvicg, whose idealistic rationalism influenced several generations of pre-World-War II French philosophers, is the author most often cited in this volume; in opposition to him, Duméry is concerned

9. *Critique et religion,* p. 227.
10. *Philosophie de la religion,* I, p. 5.
11. *Ibid.* p,. 122.

to show that theism does not oblige one to sacrifice interiority through an unwarranted leap into a Super-World. Our author accepts the fundamental orientation of phenomenology but wants to extend it further than Husserl did in any of the texts now published. Thus the most original thesis of the present book is that, in addition to Husserl's three reductions, a fourth reduction is necessary.

Duméry distinguishes his philosophy of religion from what has sometimes been called the phenomenology of religion. In the words of one of its earliest and foremost representatives, the latter is designed to "order the main groups of religious phenomena without explaining them by doctrinaire reduction in such a way that the most important aspects and viewpoints emerge from the material itself." [12] This phenomenological approach to the history of religions, whose influence has been decisive in the twentieth century, has been practiced by such masters as Otto, Van der Leeuw, Wach, and Eliade.[13] Duméry would agree with Spiegelberg's classification of this current as one of the extra-philosophical phenomenologies. According to Duméry, philosophy of religion profits from phenomenological description but its special task is to provide the basis for a normative classification of the evidence. Philosophy

12. P. D. Chantepie de la Saussaye in his *Lehrbuch der Religionsgeschichte*, quoted by Herbert Spiegelberg, *The Phenomenological Movement: A Historical Introduction* (The Hague, 1960), p. 10.

13. There is great variety in the degree to which phenomenological techniques are used as a precise method for description or intuition of essences. Phenomenology has attracted a multitude of students of religion who became dissatisfied with historicism and objectivism. A recent example of a very general sympathy with phenomenology is Edward J. Jurgi's *The Phenomenology of Religion* (Philadelphia, 1963).

seeks conditions of possibility and effects a theoretical judgment.[14] The moments of description and judgment are complementary yet distinct. Chapter V of *Critique et religion* is a highly laudatory exposition of "Phenomenological Description." In Chapter VI, "Reflective and Critical Analysis: method of discrimination," Duméry proposes to take up problems of genesis as well as those of essence and to occupy the metaphysical void left by Husserl.[15] In books published in the 1920's, Max Scheler, Kurt Stavenhagen, and Jean Héring used phenomenology to deal with the specifically philosophical issues related to religion. But for various reasons all three abandoned this line of inquiry and Duméry is the first philosopher to take it up again in its full scope. Thus Duméry is drawing on more than half a century of phenomenological attention to religion, yet he is also breaking new ground.

There are other important voices in this conversation, for it must be remembered that Duméry, a Frenchman, comes to Husserl through the mediation of Sartre and Merleau-Ponty. Husserl was hesitant to pronounce on metaphysical issues, and above all on the problem of God, yet the first two important French philosophies that he inspired are non-theistic ontologies. Neither does Duméry abstain from ontology, though he proposes a very different development on Husserl. Not the least salutary effect of this conflict among Husserl's interpreters would be a serious return to Husserl himself.

Adopting a French locution, we can say that at a certain level Duméry accepts Sartre's *problématique;* to some extent Duméry's problem is set for him by the non-theistic French phenomenologies. Though he does

14. Cf. *Critique et religion*, p. 241.
15. *Ibid.*, p. 221.

not accept Sartre's denial of theism, he does agree with Sartre that man creates meaning and value. From the perspective of the theisms that deny this creative capacity to man, Duméry is an atheist with Sartre; but Duméry is a theist vis-à-vis Sartre because he contends that a God-thing or God-object or God-idea is not the only possible God. For him, God is none of these but rather that by which they are.

Prefacing one of Duméry's books, Jean Lacroix says, "Duméry's whole originality—more traditional than one would think—is to separate modern humanism [Marxism and Sartrian existentialism] from its atheistic context." [16] In the same volume Duméry suggests that the period during which he wrote these essays was characterized by an affirmation of the radical freedom of the spirit. "Humanism has never before been pushed to this depth where the spirit appears as a freedom immanent and transcendent to empirical individuality." [17] Duméry accepts this radical humanism and says that contemporary philosophy has led him "to take up again, in a theistic context, the problem of human creativity and freedom that recent masters have believed they can resolve by dispensing with God." [18]

In the four extremely dense chapters of *The Problem of God*, Duméry presents his natural theology or doctrine of God. The first chapter has the dual purpose of first defining philosophy as critical reflection on con-

16. *Regards sur la philosophie contemporaine* (Paris, 1957), p. 8. This volume is a collection of sixty reviews written by Duméry during the period 1942–54 when he was the philosophical chronicler for a Paris Roman Catholic daily newspaper. These short perceptive essays, originally published under a pen name, are marked by an intellectual generosity that is perhaps unequaled in the philosophical literature of today.

17. *Ibid.*, p. 12.

18. *Ibid.*

crete action and then attempting to refute other approaches that either falsify religion as it is concretely lived or compromise the radical transcendence of God. Chapter Two is Duméry's reductive "argument" for the reality of God, followed by an attempt to reveal the continuity of this position with certain moments in Western philosophy. Chapters Three and Four attempt to clarify the relationship of God and the human spirit by proposing a henology (which is contrasted to objectivist ontologies) and an interpretation of various forms of human language concerning the divine.

As the above summary indicates, the final two chapters are logically dependent on Chapter Two. They explicate the relationship of the spirit to God that supposedly has already been proved. Consequently, the discussion to follow emphasizes the methodological considerations of Chapter One and especially the proof in Chapter Two. Such a procedure would recommend itself for pedagogical reasons. In this particular case, moreover, I find that the logical heart of the book is also the most difficult and raises the most problems.

By defining philosophy as critical reflection on concrete action, Duméry seeks to make a sharp distinction between philosophy and action and, at the same time, to insist that they are related. The mode of their relation assures their distinction, for philosophy is dependent on concrete action. Other terms that Duméry uses for the latter are spontaneous activity, lived experience, and practice; Husserl's natural, or thetic, attitude is equivalent in scope to Duméry's concrete action. In another context Duméry borrows Le Senne's classification of four basic types of activity: mathematics, aesthetics, morals, and religion.[19] Adopting Blondel's terminology,

19. *Philosophie de la religion*, I, p. 51.

Duméry says that action is prospective; it involves the realization of goals. Philosophical reflection, by contrast, is retrospective. It is a secondary effort of recovery that occurs, so to speak, after the fact. Philosophy follows in the wake of practice and feeds from it; philosophy "is . . . the word of life . . . not life itself." [20] There is no competition between the two domains. Action remains intact while philosophy attempts to recover and clarify its intelligible structure. Philosophy employs autonomous principles of intelligibility, order, and logic, but it is dependent upon spontaneous action to provide the material for reflection.

Since philosophy is a moment of disinterested reflection, all other human activity is transcendent to it. Because philosophers seek to discover the essential structures of human consciousness, they regard all forms of consciousness, no matter how theoretical or subjective, as modes of positivity. Of course there are distinct modes of transcendence, but for philosophy there is nothing that is not transcendent to the reflective effort. Duméry says, "lived experience . . . is always 'transcendent' to the reflective plane." (11) Consequently, it is as proper to have a problem of the relation of reason to perception as it is to have the problem of the relation of reason to faith.

An important corollary of the principle that philosophy is dependent upon lived experience is that the totality of human action and expression is open to philosophical examination. Duméry says, "by right, reflection is coextensive with the total range of human

20. *The Problem of God*, p. 5. This is the page number in the English translation; hereafter, all page references to this translation will be given in the text by means of numbers enclosed in parentheses.

action." (11) None of the human activities can be
sheltered from philosophy. This is especially important
in philosophy of religion, since with this principle
Duméry directly challenges the influential theory that
distinguishes truths of reason from truths of faith and
declares the latter impermeable to philosophy. Duméry,
however, does not deny that there are truths of faith and
he does not seek to supplant them with philosophical
surrogates. If philosophy is a critical, secondary effort, it
cannot encroach on any form of experience and, reciprocally, no legitimate barriers can be raised against it.
Again, in principle there is no more reason to challenge
philosophy's right to examine religion than there is to
challenge its right to examine perception. The issue
here is fundamental; if reflection did not have universal
extension, "there would be no philosophy of religion.
There would be no philosophy at all." (11)

Philosophy is reflection. Does this mean that all
reflection is philosophical? No. Spontaneous action
includes what Blondel called *spontaneous reflection.*
The concrete is not the realm of darkness; it is the place
of thoughtful action, or thought in act. Action is intentional, purposeful, and coherent; thus it must be informed by thought. The distinctive feature of spontaneous reflection is that it is prospective. Examples can be
cited from the whole range of action: a housekeeper
planning her marketing, a chemist preparing an experi-
ment, a moral sage formulating maxims of conduct.
According to Duméry, such thought is in the service of
action and "does not know itself as reflection." (6)

Moreover, thought in action has its own rules. Its
truth or adequacy does not depend upon philosophical
justification. Let us take an example relevant to the
themes of this book. It may be claimed that philosophy

can combat idolatry by demonstrating that there is but one God. Duméry would insist that even if this were so, God may be worshiped properly by a religious man who is completely ignorant of philosophy. Concrete religion, Christianity for example, has practical injunctions against idolatry. If philosophy is really to be *of* religion, what it says about idolatry must be grounded in the concrete religious phenomena relevant to idolatry.

Of course, this position does not preclude the possibility that the same person may be a believer and also a philosopher. It only seeks to clarify the roles. The distinction between spontaneous faith and philosophically understood faith is legitimate and helpful so long as the former is not regarded as religiously inferior. To do so would be to turn religion into gnosticism, where salvation is reserved for the intellectual elite. According to Duméry, faith includes knowledge, awareness, and intelligibility; concrete religion is not irrational or anti-intellectual. If there are such cases, it is because the religious impulse, and consequently man, has been betrayed. Philosophical understanding of religion is valuable and adds a new dimension of awareness. But to require such awareness of the religious man makes an idolatry of reason. To fabricate a religion of reason is to introduce a false positivity into philosophy.

But what assures the continuity of prospective and philosophical reflection? What guarantees that philosophical reflection actually has to do with concrete lived experience? Duméry answers these questions by pointing out the immediate pre-reflective consciousness of self that accompanies all conscious acts. It is the mid-point between the two orders of reflection and functions as a bridge. Duméry says that philosophy "is only the technically ordered awareness of" the reflection of the concrete subject. (24, n. 22) Philosophy is the rational exercise through which reason comes into possession of itself; it "is nothing other than . . . reason become fully conscious of itself, master of its criteria." (24, n. 22) Philosophy is the deepening of the immediate self-consciousness which is the coincidence of the *ratio essendi* and the *ratio cognoscendi;* it is a reflexive movement that reveals consciousness' mode of being. Philosophy is not introspective knowledge of self, nor is it what the Medievals called a second intention, which has the same noetic structure as a first intention but is directed toward the subject as agent. Duméry is squarely in the French tradition of "l'analyse réflexive" which goes back to Descartes and has been one of the central themes of French philosophy throughout modern times.[21] This tradition accounts in large measure for the peculiar French response to Husserl that we have in Sartre, Merleau-Ponty, and Ricoeur.[22]

21. Cf. Pierre Thévenaz, *What is Phenomenology?*, ed. James M. Edie (Chicago, 1962), especially pp. 113–32.

22. I considered writing "reflexion" and "reflexive" in the translation, but decided against it because consistency would lead to some easily imaginable orthographical barbarisms. In any case, the reader should refrain from associating "reflection" and "reflective," as they are used here, with optical phenomena or sage cogitation. A reflexive relation of identity or coincidence, such as we have in grammar, mathematics, or logic, is more pertinent to philosophical reflection as Duméry understands it. It is interesting to note that William James regarded the optical phenomenon of total reflection (in 1907 James wrote "reflexion") as "a good symbol of the relation between abstract ideas and concrete reality. . . . Both worlds are real, of course, and interact; but they interact only at their boundary." (*Pragmatism: A New Name for Some Old Ways of Thinking,* New York, 1907, pp. 127–28.) As usual, James's simile is illuminating, and it clarifies an important idea. James shares this idea with the French tradition mentioned above, and the idea remains. But the rules of spelling change, and out of respect for *Webster* I must be content with writing "reflection."

Philosophy is criticism as well as reflection. What does this imply? The reader would not be wrong in seeing certain affinities with Kant's critical philosophy. Philosophy, as criticism, is an inquiry that begins from a given experience or body of knowledge and seeks the intelligible conditions of its possibility. It recovers the laws immanent to action by establishing a rational transcendental logic that necessarily applies to all phenomena. Philosophy is no super-science that discovers a new world of entities. It is limited to a study of the forms of human consciousness. The philosophy of religion does not study the religious capacity or instinct; that is a task for psychology. Philosophy is transcendental inquiry that distinguishes the several levels of consciousness and defines their roles. Concrete affirmations are made by the living subject and philosophy institutes an examination of their intelligible coherence and necessity. Philosophy decides whether, from its point of view, an idea is affirmable and practicable. "The philosopher limits himself to stating the rule for choice, the meaning and scope of engagement." (13) He then puts the idea back in the hands of the living subject.

Thus philosophy does perform a certain mode of judgment. It is, however, strictly limited to the plane of transcendental reflection. It can reveal logical contradictions; it can show when a level of consciousness is being asked to perform a role foreign to it; it can spot confusions and ambiguity in expression. It cannot do more. If an idea or expression withstands philosophical scrutiny, it can be recommended as affirmable. But there may be several affirmable alternatives in a given situation. It remains for the concrete subject to choose, to engage values and ideas, to act.

Finally, we should mention a difficulty with Duméry's

conception of philosophy, which may or may not involve only his terminology. His position is based on the distinction between action and reflection; yet if that distinction is maintained rigorously philosophy cannot be called an activity. Where, then, does philosophy fit into Duméry's ontology? Several times he lapses and refers to the act of philosophizing and the intense effort of attention that it requires. What can such statements mean? Is a radical reconsideration of the action-reflection distinction called for? This problem will come up in a different form in the discussion of Chapter Four; in both cases we have to be content with mentioning it. If, for the moment, we can regard this as a terminological problem, there is a solution compatible with the position we have attempted to expose in the preceding paragraphs. "Action" can be the general term to comprehend all conscious experience. The two fundamental modes of consciousness or action are "prospection" and "retrospection." The latter, of course, is philosophy.

Let us now turn to Duméry's arguments against certain other approaches to the philosophy of religion. It is easy to anticipate his objections to the famous disjunction between the God of the philosophers and the God of the faithful. He regards this as a bogus problem which has arisen because philosophers, whether religious or not, have failed to acknowledge the reflective, critical function of philosophy. The idea of God originates in religion and the philosopher must seek it there if he wants to deal with the living God and not with an ideal fabrication. Duméry says bluntly, "the God of philosophers is from the start a theft and a blunder." (7) He continues, "there is only one God . . . a God that religion worships and that philosophy must take into consideration, as it does any other value. . . . the affirmation of God is a work of free and spontaneous consciousness. The work of philosophical reflection is to state in what way this affirmation is coherent and obligatory, or on the contrary, vain and superfluous." (7–8) Duméry's philosophy solves this problem by not letting it arise.

But in addition to the negative solution of the problem, Duméry also tries to show, from the inside, that there are insuperable difficulties with any objectivist approach. He chooses to discuss explicitly the philosophies that claim an explanatory or causal scheme can be used to demonstrate the existence of God. Duméry answers that the notion of cause is applicable only in an order where the cause and the effect share the same mode of being. Consequently, he argues that the God discovered at the end of a chain of explanations or causes is never more than the final member of the chain, and thus is homogeneous with the inferior links. Such a God is a thing, an object, an idea, but not the radically transcendent living God. In two places, Duméry poses a dilemma for the advocate of such an argument: either the final link is like the others (in series with them), and a God worthy of the name is not attained; or the final link is unlike the others, and although God is attained, the chain is broken and there is no genuine proof. (29 and 34) He suggests that an objectivist approach is convincing only because it implicitly employs an approach similar to his own. (29) He is, however, willing to admit later (71) that the argument through causes can be accepted if a strictly metaphysical, as opposed to natural, notion of cause is employed. The doctrine of analogy has been developed to complement the objectivist demonstrations of God's existence. In the final part of *Foi et institution* Duméry, referring to some of his Thomist critics, specifies in what sense he also accepts analogy as a philosophical tool. He maintains that from the beginning henology contains what is true in the doctrine of analogy; consequently, it does not run the risk of introducing analogy too late.

In his refutation of objectivist theism, Duméry appeals only to the nature of the human subject. Several times he refers to the fully developed philosophical anthropology found in the first part of *Philosophie de la religion*. Nevertheless, *The Problem of God* is perfectly comprehensible by itself because the basic feature of human subjectivity is revealed by means of the dialectical analysis of the objectivist approach. The nerve of Duméry's objection is contained in the following sentence: "Whether the philosopher is aware of it or not, the notions he connects hold together by means of the living Cogito, and the latter, instead of being a pure form, is an act which expresses itself at different levels." (30) All significations, including the most abstract and general principles, are products of this act. Thus there is no way to God that leads directly from a system of ideas. The acting subject, rather than God, is at the end of any chain of ideas. ". . . between an explanatory series and the Absolute, there is the infinite distance from the reflective to the concrete, an impassable distance for any other initiative than that of the acting subject." (33) In another context, Duméry says that because philosophy has failed to see the correlation between the human creation of essences and the radical or henological transcendence of God, it has oscillated between a thing-ish theism and an atheistic humanism.[23] If these two propositions are really correlative, it is indeed

23. *Philosophie de la religion*, I, p. 66.

legitimate to refute a theism by exposing the anthropological doctrine it implies.

Duméry's case can be summarized in the following terms. Radical humanism, of which phenomenology with its series of three reductions is an example, shows that the acting subject creates significations. This result poses a double difficulty for objectivist theism. First, God can no longer be the seat of ideas and determinations. They are "located" at the level of the human subject. If there is a God, he must be trans-determinate. Second, theism cannot ignore that on this side of the divine there is a non-objectifiable reality that is not a determination, namely, the human subject. Since reduction leads us to an act rather than to an ultimate idea, a proof of God cannot be simply another argument similar to those that are proper to other objects.

Consequently, if we are not to lapse into notionalism, we must attempt to advance beyond the Cogito. A series of reductions can be supplemented only by another reduction; but is that suggestion thinkable? A fourth reduction is the possibility Duméry explores in Chapter Two.

The purpose of Chapter Two is to present the reductive argument for the existence of God. Before examining this argument it will be helpful to underline the very precise limits Duméry sets for his natural theology. We have already seen that the doctrines of the Absolute and the subject form a metaphysical prolegomenon to the doctrinal studies in philosophy of religion. Consequently, God will be the object of several types of inquiry, and our immediate task is to show what Duméry means by a strictly metaphysical study of the idea of God.

We are told in the Preface that *The Problem of God*

is an "attempt to see if the idea of God can withstand *critical dissolution.*" (lv) This approach, which is clearly different from the other possibilities mentioned there, is specified and defended in the Conclusion to *Critique et religion.* We are told that the metaphysical approach, or the procedure of reduction, is the most radical and general type of reflection. With the technique of reduction one distinguishes the basic sense of the idea of God from the various representations that accompany it. Moreover, only this approach will appear cogent to those critics of religion who attempt to explain away religious experience as "illusion or mystification." [24] In other terms, a metaphysical prolegomenon to a philosophy *of religion* is demanded because "presenting the idea of God by means of the concrete attitudes of the religious man . . . is a useful but not sufficient approach." [25] Duméry concludes that we must "begin by a simple critique of the notion of the Absolute, in its relation to the aspiration of consciousness, independent of the religious representations that express it." [26]

It seems strange that a philosopher who has argued so brilliantly in behalf of a philosophy that keeps contact with the concrete should set himself such an austere task concerning God. Is there an inconsistency here? No, I think not. Though Duméry uses technical terms and though he attempts to put abstract concepts into logically impeccable arguments, his approach is not guilty of the formalism or objectivism or positivism he disputes. For he intends to make a critique of the notion of the Absolute as it is related "to the aspiration of consciousness." Duméry believes he specifies the real

24. *Critique et religion,* p. 226.
25. *Ibid.*
26. *Ibid.,* p. 227.

aspiration of consciousness in the philosophical anthropology developed in *Philosophie de la religion*. The
philosophy of the human subject as such is systematically related to the philosophies of the several concrete
activities; it is a more general science worked out on the
basis of sciences whose scope is smaller. Though it is
highly abstract, it is nothing other than the explicit
formulation of the principles operative in the derivative
sciences. Duméry will attempt to construct a natural
theology by exploiting the very movement of reflection
that is begun but not achieved at the stage of philosophical anthropology.

He is aware that a doctrine of God based directly and
exclusively on religious evidence would, to religion's
adversary, appear to beg the question. On the other
hand, to put the issue in non-religious terms seems, to
the advocate of religion, merely to change the subject
and miss the point. Is there a way out of this impasse?
Duméry contends that there is. He suggests that religion,
as a human activity, is an ensemble of conscious acts.
As such, with respect to a general philosophy of consciousness, religion is in the same position as all other
human activities. As a form of expression and representation, religion uses the same levels and functions of
consciousness as do art, empirical sciences, and mathematics. Consequently, a philosophy of human consciousness as such should have the right to tell us whether
religion, an activity directed toward the divine, is a
misuse of consciousness.

If Duméry is right, the advocate of religion cannot
consistently deny that, from one perspective, religion is
an ensemble of conscious acts; he must admit that
Duméry proposes at least a legitimate way of broaching
the problem of God. Similarly, if the denial of the

genuineness of religion is to be more than an unfounded assertion, religion's adversary must agree that it is legitimate to pose the issue in terms of a philosophy of consciousness. As a philosopher, moreover, he is obliged to defend a theory of consciousness that accounts for all the forms of consciousness, even certain aberrational forms, including, perhaps, religion.

Duméry's tactics in dealing with his opponents are based on the approach mentioned above. In Chapter II of *Critique et religion,* he attempts to show that a philosophy which explains away religion has a false understanding of consciousness as such. Thus the reasons for its misconception of religion will also lead it to give an inadequate interpretation of scientific activity. On the other hand, Duméry challenges certain inept ways of regarding the traditional proofs for the existence of God because they fail to grasp the nature of intelligible determinations.

If the nature of consciousness is to be the basis for a proof of God's existence, it follows that the reflective movement can begin with any conscious act whatsoever. If it does begin with a religious act, for the purposes of the argument its specifically religious characteristics can be ignored. Duméry says that a philosophical proof of God is possible because God is "immanent to the reason and to all the powers of the concrete subject . . . [and] *is really operative in all consciousness.*" (24)

In certain passages of *The Problem of God,* Duméry seems to blur the distinction between metaphysics and philosophy of religion. (17 and 39) In the analysis which follows I will assume, however, that he is doing metaphysics and will build up my interpretation and evaluation accordingly.

When Duméry gives his proof of God the name "reduction," he makes clear the historical associations involved. (40) The reference to Husserl emphasizes that reduction is a movement in several stages; the reference to Leibniz' "apperception" indicates that reduction is a mode of awareness. By insisting that reduction works within concrete experience (40) yet keeps its distance from it, Duméry preserves the element of *epoché* or suspension so important to Husserl. Our author reveals, however, that he is frankly interested in going beyond phenomenological description toward metaphysics when he says that reduction is "a movement that seeks to pass through the different levels of consciousness in order to secure, step by step, their foundation." (40)

Duméry is aware of the hazards involved in this approach to metaphysics. He admits that the "difficulty with reduction is that out of respect for the nature of experience . . . it must maintain the solidarity (while distinguishing them) of subject and object." (40–41) The tension alluded to here arises because even though philosophy is concerned with the pure field of transcendental consciousness, it is a consciousness that has reality only insofar as it is *of* something, that is, incarnated and involved in the world. The progressive analysis of the subject "implies a corresponding promotion of the object." (41) The unity of consciousness and world is maintained wherever it obtains; consequently, we have to do with a reflective analysis that never is faced with the insoluble problem of establishing contact between consciousness and world. The reason is that contact is never interrupted.

The primary unit of reality for Duméry is a concrete experience that involves all of man's powers. Philosophy makes distinctions and constructs terminologies, but these should never be allowed to displace the unity upon which they depend. "The philosopher, like the scientist, engages in but a single type of construction; he elaborates complicated and subtle instruments in order to bring to light the implications of the real . . . " (61) Each of the levels of consciousness is named and some are said to be dependent on others. It would be wrong, however, to regard consciousness as a composite whole made up of discrete entities; the model of a tower of blocks is not appropriate. Duméry prefers to speak of functions and roles and attitudes of consciousness. For example, he refuses to say that the decision to affirm God is option or judgment but not both. Such a dilemma arises only when the doctrine of the faculties of will and intelligence is misused by turning an "academic distinction into a metaphysical distinction. For us, both option and judgment are referred to the spiritual totality, whose different functions interpenetrate." (57) Consciousness itself produces the diverse orders while maintaining a global and undivided attitude. Philosophical reduction is only a reflective recovery of what is already there.

It still must be explained how reduction, which deals only with transcendental consciousness, can avoid being subjectivistic. Duméry answers that exclusive attention can be given to the subjective without falling into subjectivism so long as one remembers that the subject under scrutiny is the subject *of* full concrete experience. Concrete experience, characterized by subject-object unity, ranges from the relative passivity of some sensory experiences to the high degree of activity involved in scientific and aesthetic discernment. The thought involved in concrete experience is prospective and, rather than clarifying the subject-object relationship, presupposes it. According to Duméry, the task of clarification falls to philosophy. His project of clarification could be stated in the following manner. The concrete is a realm of inter-action; or, what we call action is the result of the subject's act in the world. If concrete experience is a subject-object unity, each component must contribute something specific. Therefore, one way of clarifying the relationship is to disclose what one of these contributions is. Duméry's project, and incidentally his interpretation of Husserl's program, is to discover the act of the subject.

Philosophy is the reflective consideration of real experience. The philosopher has before him the entire content of the experience, but as it is seen from the perspective of consciousness alone. The object remains, but now simply as correlate of consciousness. At each stage of reduction, that which the subject contributes is discriminated. The relative activity and passivity of consciousness is ascertained. Each succeeding level of consciousness is shown to be the foundation of the one which precedes it. Thus as we move through the stages of reduction we come closer and closer to the fundamental act of consciousness, the aspect of experience that can be attributed only to it. If the movement is successful, we will discover in what sense the subject is beyond its object; in other words, we will come to regard the subject as objectifying.

It will be helpful for us to note what this position does not claim. Although the unique activity of consciousness is discovered, it is not claimed that this act has reality independently of the full concrete situation. Consciousness is actual only by being conscious of an object. The reflective clarification of consciousness operates within and is dependent upon real experience. Likewise, reduction of the objective or passive implies no negative judgment as to the existence of that which is other than consciousness. Reduction is a very carefully directed inquiry into one mode of being and nothing is affirmed or denied about other realities.

Duméry is convinced that a metaphysics of consciousness has peculiar advantages. First, since its point of departure is the immediate self-awareness that accompanies all conscious acts, it has an indubitable starting point. The difficulty of going from thought to being never arises because consciousness is regarded as a mode of being. As we have mentioned before, immediate self-awareness is the coincidence of thought and being. A metaphysics of consciousness seems to be a realizable project since philosophy itself is merely a continuation or prolongation of consciousness, the mode of being to which it has privileged access, to which, indeed, it is originally identical. Second, this metaphysics can be a radically critical enterprise of thought. Duméry does not deny the so-called empirical element in all experience, but he contends that empiricism extrapolated into an ontology is a mistake since it fails to raise the specifically metaphysical questions. Similarly, he contends that some forms of realism are inadequate because they enter forthwith into a study of being and leave the meaning of being uncriticized. A philosophy that discovers consciousness to be the creator of all signification, including the meaning of being, is the only philosophy that can carry out a radical clarification of its foundations. In short, the advantage of a metaphysics of consciousness is that it can protect both its flanks; its starting point in pre-reflective consciousness is indubitable, and it can reveal the foundation of all its principles.

Since Duméry introduces Section II of Chapter Two with the words, "This demonstration having been made," (52) we can assume that the reductive proof is found in Section I. Let us follow its steps. The first three stages of the reductive movement, in which Duméry thinks he is merely taking over the results of Husserl's analyses, reveal the various elements of a full conscious act. The first reduction, which removes us from the domain of natural fact, focuses the domain of meaning as such. At the next stage particular meanings are reduced in order to disclose general meanings. The third reduction shows that in its activity of constituting essences the transcendental subject is creative. For convenience, let us call the three levels now discerned the sensible, the rational, and the transcendental. Duméry's originality is to propose a fourth reduction, a reduction to God. (In this book Duméry uses the terms God, Absolute, the One, pure Unity, and Pure Act interchangeably.) He contends that in the first three reductions we employ a principle of reflection that can be arrested at the transcendental subject only by an arbitrary decision. What is this principle and how does it operate?

The principle is that as long as the reducible remains, reduction must continue. Most often Duméry says the reducible is the multiple; other terms used are passive, dependent, and finite. The levels of particular and general meanings, the sensible and the rational, can serve as examples. These levels are characterized by multiplicity because they have a plurality of meanings and each meaning is distinguishable only through its relationship to the other meanings at its level. Of course the level itself is a form of unity; it is a system of reciprocally determining meanings. The following is perhaps the most explicit expression of the principle that motivates the reductive movement. "To the extent that, within a given, I succeed in discriminating variable elements and, in contrast, a common principle which invariably is found in all the cases, I am authorized to set the first aside so as to better exhibit the second. But this procedure, judged legitimate at the outset, cannot lose its legitimacy along the way." (43)

The several degrees of unity are not only specified; they are also put in hierarchical order. Duméry holds that the prospective consciousness already knows how to distinguish the various levels. Philosophy can develop a theory of noetic levels because it discerns the differences in quality that are already constituted in real experience. (55) The unity of the levels that are tainted by multiplicity is relative, unstable, and needs to be founded by a superior unity. The dependence of the sensible upon the intelligible can be directly discerned, and though the intelligible never appears as such, it can justifiably be posited. (43) The successive foundations that this process secures are increasingly less rich than concrete experience but at the same time influence larger and larger domains. The relationship between the sensible and rational levels again provides a clear example.

Duméry uses the above interpretation of the stages of reduction as a base from which to launch his proposal that the movement must continue until a pure unity, an irreducible, is discovered. Specifically, the demonstrable multiplicity of the transcendental invites and demands the reduction to God. Thus it appears that he has adhered to the original agreement not to use religious evidence in constructing the proof. Duméry has merely proposed that when the effort of reductive reflection is considered from a certain point of view it can be seen to contain a rational exigency that does not achieve equilibrium short of the Absolute.

If the principle of the reductive movement is accepted, it seems that the above proof is complete and valid. We must, however, draw attention to some passages that introduce new elements. For the reductive approach, the disclosure of God as pure Unity is *simultaneous* with the realization that the transcendental is multiple. (105, 128) The only conscious act drawn on is one in which "the intelligible fulfills the function of its order." (58) Other texts suggest that there is a different activity which I shall call the experience of contestability. Duméry says that man can know that he is the artisan of knowledge and the constructer of relationships and still be terribly frustrated, because his freedom has the capacity to undo what it has done and because he has more profound aspirations.[27] The frustration mentioned here does not arise merely because of man's incomplete knowledge of the world, for it is the nature of such knowledge to be continually revised and augmented. For example, nothing is more natural than that I should contest my present knowledge of a given perceptual object; and such contesting is entirely compatible with Duméry's theory of consciousness. The appropriate motivation for such contestation would be additional empirical evidence. But empirical evidence alone is not a sufficient condition for the other mode of contesting indicated above; other factors must be introduced before we can understand the notions of "frustration," "freedom," and "aspiration." Whereas for the first

27. *Critique et religion,* p. 65.

type of contestation we can say that no given determination is adequate to the object, it is more correct to say that in the second case man discovers that nothing determinate satisfies him.

In this Introduction we cannot explore all the ramifications of the problem of the phenomena of radical contestation. We will have to be satisfied with posing some of the questions it gives rise to and suggesting a way of resolving the difficulty. The questions concern the relation of contestability to Duméry's anthropology, to the reductive proof, and to the intention of *The Problem of God.*

Duméry uses a series of three reductions to present his philosophical anthropology. Does this anthropology, designed to clarify all human activities, comprehend the activity of contesting? Perhaps it is incorrect to call it a form of activity since, as the following text indicates, it has affinities with the experience of nothingness that other contemporary authors have accentuated.

> . . . when it is a question of breaking with the highest order, so as to suspend it from that by which it is, the risk becomes total. One must be ready to challenge all that one has, all that one is, all being. . . . This attitude is so daring that at this point it threatens all objective security. It severely upsets established habits. . . . [Man's] demand always goes beyond all that he attains and forces him to proceed further. This is a sign that an infinite dynamism works in him, fading his joys, annihilating his conquests, perpetually placing what he has and is at a distance from what he desires. (57, 59)

Nevertheless, these phrases refer to a concrete experience which Duméry's anthropology, if adequate, should be able to criticize fully. The three reductions disclose the sensible, the rational, and finally the intelligible levels of consciousness. Since contesting, however, pre-supposes intelligible determination and stands in a negative relation to it, it appears that the series of three reductions is inadequate.

Perhaps, then, the experience of contestability makes it necessary to extend the series of reductions. After all, it would have made no sense to speak of the subject as contester until his function as determiner had been revealed. But there are difficulties with this suggestion as well. The reductions isolate the successive levels of consciousness and arrive at the intelligible act. Contesting can be accommodated in the series only if we found it on a higher level of consciousness. The third reduction has revealed the one-multiple, the pure Cogito in correlation with the world; this is the most general of all relationships. Supposedly the next step, if there is one, is not to another level of consciousness but to pure Unity. These remarks are enough to show that Duméry at least owes us some clarification.

What is the relationship of contestability to the reductive proof? Apparently the proof can be stated without taking it into account. Yet Duméry asserts, "One *must* be ready to challenge all that one has, all that one is, all being, *in order to* discover the single incontestable that depends only upon itself and whose only foundation is its spontaneity: the Absolute, the One, God." (57, italics added) It appears that the author again owes us an explanation. For it is not clear how contestability complements or completes the reductive proof; and on the other hand, Duméry does not develop an alternative proof on the basis of the capacity for contesting.

Finally, is the use of the experience of contestability compatible with the purpose of the book? Our previous questions dictate our first response. The criticism of the idea of God presupposes an adequate philosophy of consciousness. If, however, with contestability we have found an aspect of experience that is refractory to Duméry's analysis of consciousness, then we lack one necessary condition for developing the critique of God. More specifically, it should be noted that contestability is a particular type of experience, whereas the original proposal was to make a proof for God that could start from any conscious act whatsoever. In fact, it seems that in the following passage Duméry is in danger of betraying his purpose.

> . . . concerning the Absolute, philosophy has no other task than to criticize *the way thought* (or living spirituality) *proceeds when it wants to prove the existence of God to itself.* . . . the spirit succeeds in proving God only by surmounting the sensible and the intelligible, by understanding that they are not self-sufficient. But that is nothing other than the reduction lived and thought before philosophy learned to name and formulate it. . . . without the effective act that guides and sustains this effort, secondary reflection would find itself without an object. (61–62)

If the above is philosophy's only task concerning the Absolute, then it seems that Duméry has left the peculiarly metaphysical task aside. Moreover, it must be asked if a proof of God is an essential part of the religious life. Certainly, many people in our time have attempted to resolve the question of God by asking whether the sensible and intelligible orders are self-sufficient. But it is unwise for Duméry to suggest that this approach is necessary or universal. It is the approach adopted by a widespread type of contemporary spirituality, and by emphasizing it Duméry may be fulfilling a certain apologetic task. Such considerations, however, are irrelevant to the philosophical problem at issue.

Obviously, the difficulties raised by contesting are serious. In our opinion, however, they can be treated in a way that leaves Duméry's fundamental position intact. We can note first that in a metaphysical argument contesting need not be presented as a special mode of experience that strains or breaks the anthropology already discussed. For, if contesting is a distinguishable mode of human experience it has a structure, an intelligibility, that can be clarified by Duméry's intentional analysis. Contesting and other activities employ the same levels of consciousness. Each form of activity, contesting not excepted, is distinguished by its object. The question, then, is whether contesting has an object, whether its intention is well-founded or illusory. Next it must be pointed out that we can disregard the experience of radical contestation and still show that the Cogito, rather than being a determination, is a determining act. Finally, if radical contesting is one mode of experience among others it should not and cannot be the sole experiential basis of the argument for the reality of God. In other words, with respect to the transcendental inquiry we are conducting in *The Problem of God,* all modes of experience must be regarded as equivalent. Even though the status of the experience of contesting depends upon the success or failure of the reductive movement to the Absolute, philosophical reflection must ignore the specific characteristics of contesting. We can say that if the reductive movement is successful we should expect to find the experience of contesting, that is, a living intention specifically oriented toward God. In short, if and only if it can be shown that the one-multiple implies the One do we have a *philo-*

sophical justification of the activity by which the one-multiple intends the One.

In the third section of Chapter Two, Duméry attempts to bring out the connections between his position and some of the great traditions in Western philosophy. These brilliant pages, which show acquaintance with the best contemporary scholarship, reveal a profound understanding of several philosophies and a sensitivity to the subtlety of the problems involved. With no imperialistic motives, Duméry sincerely tries to show in what respects St. Thomas, St. Bonaventure, and certain advocates of the ontological argument are henologists *implicités*. The tradition of negative theology, with its Plotinian roots, is operative throughout the discussion; the long note on pages 74–75 gives us indispensable clarifications of Duméry's attitude toward it.

In Chapters Three and Four Duméry turns to a new task. He has shown that the category of the Absolute withstands criticism, that is, "a trans-ordinal Absolute has been proved; the reality of transcendence has already been brought to light." (80) We now move forward to elaborate a well-founded position. The task is to criticize the scheme of transcendence; this involves asking if there are justifiable ways to think and talk about the Absolute.

Section 1 is directed largely against Brunschvicg's objection that any transcendence whatsoever involves exteriority and the destruction of the spirit. Duméry's response is that the dilemma of a realist exteriority and an idealist interiority is no longer to be feared since the creativity of the spirit and the correlative trans-ordinal character of God have been demonstrated. The metaphors of the beyond and depth have their particular advantages and liabilities; but both of them are imaginative schemes that stand in need of criticism. (81–83) Duméry's positive answer to Brunschvicg's challenge is to reformulate the relation of the spirit to God. (91–93) The integrity of the spirit is maintained because the spirit is a limited freedom and it is through God that the spirit has the possibility to be. Duméry repeats an argument from Chapter Two which shows that when the transcendental order is made ultimate and impersonal, personality is either unfounded or illusory. (83–84) Since the spirit is dependent, it is legitimate, and even necessary, for it to be related to a transcendent so long as this transcendent is not an obstacle from an inferior order but rather the trans-ordinal that allows the spirit to create the orders.

By making the transcendental impersonal and monistic and refusing to go beyond it to a radically transcendent Absolute, Brunschvicg joins a large company of modern thinkers. Kant, according to Duméry, discovered the transcendental and declared it to be monistic. Later philosophers, insofar as they followed Kant's understanding of the transcendental, were correct in denying the Absolute. Duméry contends that by showing the elements of plurality in the transcendental he has revived the possibility of affirming the Absolute. He has indicated that in subsequent studies he will take up the historical and systematic aspects of this issue.

Duméry is not unaware of the strengths of an ontology of being such as Gilson's. There is, nevertheless, an overriding reason which leads him to propose a henology instead. He contends that a henology can respect the transcendence and sovereignty of God without introducing subsequent correctives. Duméry is especially sensitive to the dangers of the doctrine of analogy, for example, in its Suarezian version. But we must ask whether Duméry's henology is really an improvement. For it would be easy to scan the pages of *The Problem of God* and gather a fistful of terms applied to God. He is called "source," "pure energy," "motion," "fount," etc. Does Duméry not commit the same fault as his adversary? I think not. A corollary of the henological proof of God is that human language to express the God-spirit relationship is necessary. Once God's radical transcendence is shown, the entire apparatus of human expressivity can be directed to him, and this is what occurs in a concrete religion. Duméry challenges positive theology because, using uncriticized human concepts, it offers a proof for God and afterwards supplements it with a philosophy of language that protects the divine prerogatives. Consequently, a simple attack on Duméry's language about God is misplaced; the critic should attempt to find a weakness in the interpretation of the levels of human consciousness as an ascending movement toward Unity.

Some explanation of Duméry's use of the term "conversion" may be helpful. (94–97) In henology, conversion is in polar relationship to procession. It is the philosophical act of noetic purification and clarification. Procession should be paired with action, and conversion with reflection; consequently, conversion is dependent upon and in the service of procession. There may be a parallel between religious conversion and philosophical conversion, but they should not be confused. In henological terms, the whole of concrete religion must be called procession. Duméry does speak of religious conversion but we are prevented from confusing it with philosophical conversion or purification since religion is defined as "the *active* discovery of God

as source and end." (103, italics added) It is important
to remember that Duméry is thinking of Husserl as well
as of Plotinus when he characterizes philosophy as
purification and ascesis. (47) The danger of assuming
that Duméry adopts a Plotinian position when he uses
Plotinian language is brought out clearly by Jean
Trouillard's observation that "Plotinus is a torment to
those who are fond of clear-cut oppositions. . . . In
particular, it is clear that if one makes an adequate
distinction between philosophy and spirituality, neo-
platonism becomes incomprehensible." [28] Yet if there is
any distinction that Duméry must keep clear, it is the
one between living spirituality and philosophical reflection. Duméry is using Plotinian language for his
own special purposes; even if there are occasional slips
of expression that appear to muddle the distinction between philosophy and religion, the reader should first
attempt to understand the passage in light of the project
of thought the author has announced. Perhaps he betrays his project, or perhaps it is not realizable; at any
rate, we should avoid unnecessary misinterpretations.

Chapter Three outlined a henology whose function
is to preserve the integrity proper to the spirit and to
God. There, immanentism and extrinsicism were the
errors to be avoided. Chapter Four attacks agnosticism
and anthropomorphism by developing a negative theology that justifies man's attempt to express his relationship to God.

Agnostics contend that human claims to knowledge
of God are futile and conclude that any positive religion
is a deception. Duméry accepts the contention and

28. Jean Trouillard, *La Purification plotinienne* (Paris, 1955),
p. 204.

denies the conclusion. For him, description of God is out of the question since God is trans-determinate and that by which determination is possible. Determination is valid for the determinable but "unknowing persists where unknowability exists." (114) Nonetheless, since an actual and well-defined relationship of the spirit to God has been proved, it is not necessary to follow agnosticism's counsel to remain mute. As on so many other points, Duméry shows that the traditional dilemma can and must be rejected. In this case, he says that rather than describing God himself we must try "to recover, at the plane of criticism, the meaning and value of the relation of the mind to God." (101) It is impossible to get inside God but man can come toward God; he can "live consciously the relation of the spirit to the One . . . by instituting the series of real approaches by which the spirit detects, interprets, and assumes this relationship." (104–105)

Let us note that the philosophical task is modified when the problem is to criticize the schemes that are created to express man's relationship to the divine. Whereas justifying the category of the Absolute had to be a critique of the structure of consciousness as such, examining the various schemes of expression puts philosophy in direct contact with the concrete effort by which the spirit tends toward God. For philosophy, "there is no better knowledge of God than the methodical deciphering of spiritual experience." (113–114)

Duméry exemplifies such deciphering with a discussion of the divine attributes. Philosophy interprets the attribute as "the notion in which the result of a reductive intention is inscribed." (105) The attributes are classified according to the levels of consciousness to which they belong. Certain among them—simplicity, unity, and spontaneity—are in a privileged position since they are integrally related to the reductive movement itself. (105–106) Other attributes must be reduced. To reduce them means to specify the order of consciousness to which they belong and then to determine in what respect they are "valid beyond even the notion of order," thereby liberating "the irreducible part of each one of them." (110) In other words, the various attributes are regarded as moments in a process of unification, of movement toward pure Unity.

Duméry's two-part response to agnosticism can be summarily formulated as follows. The human spirit is related to the unspeakable One and it can speak this relationship. The so-called attributes of God form part of this speech. Section II of the chapter is devoted to showing that it is necessary and proper for the human spirit to be the organ of this speaking. (113–116) A striking assertion that illustrates Duméry's position is his claim that "mystery comes from us who make the screen, not from God who is pure light. . . . God is the simple that we complicate, the One that we render 'complex,' the Absolute that we 'relativize.' " (63) n. 24)

Several of Duméry's critics have charged him with blurring the distinction between religion and philosophy and making philosophy a sort of gnostic religion. Seemingly, the following sentence is evidence in favor of the charge. "When the spirit is understood as relation to God, religion and spirituality are identified . . ." (102) If Duméry's conception of philosophy is accepted, however, this sentence is not vulnerable. For him, philosophy is reflection and not a form of spirituality. Nonetheless, does not the identification of religion and spirituality undermine the uniqueness of religion? There are at least three interpretations of this assertion which show such fear to be groundless. Religion is identical with spirituality insofar as the religious act employs the same noetic structures used in all other acts of consciousness. Religion is one of the activities of the human spirit. A second interpretation is that religion embraces all spiritual acts that explicitly involve the relation to God. Finally, when the spirit is defined, through metaphysical argument, as relation to God, there can be no spiritual act that does not involve God. In this case, even though religion may be the activity that explicitly attempts to express the relationship to God, all other acts are related to God in the sense that they are dependent on him. This interpretation allows for the specificity of religion but preserves the irrecusable and permanent presence of God to all acts.

Two important points are considered in the final section. Though Duméry will not say as a philosopher that God is a person, he does not mean that God is impersonal. "If, as we believe, the spirit personalizes or singularizes itself at the intelligible plane, the One, from which it proceeds, cannot be infra-personal, but rather is trans-personal." (120) This position, which has striking parallels with the position Tillich adopts in his famous exchange with Einstein,[29] prevents anthropomorphism while preserving the essence of religion.

The relation of God to person-hood is one aspect of the more general problem of the nature of God's assistance to man. It is a question of knowing how a genuine human freedom opening onto an unbounded future can be maintained without confusing the divine and the human. Deifying human reason ignores its ambiguity and plurality; making God a Super-Person puts him in

29. Cf. Paul Tillich, *Theology and Culture*, ed. Robert C. Kimball (New York, 1959).

competition with man. Is there a third alternative? Duméry answers affirmatively. God is the permanent presence by means of which the spirit creates the orders of meaning and value; God animates human action without becoming a part of the series of orders. St. Augustine wrote *Deus interior intimo meo* and Schleiermacher regarded the relation to the divine as the mid-point through which all human consciousness passes. Duméry is in concert with them when he says that "the slightest effective initiative and the least reflective act pass at each instant through this hidden center [the liaison of the spirit to God] from whence surges the originary spark that, at our level, bursts into light and love, thought and will." (124)

It is to be regretted that the only reference in this book to a philosopher from the United States is a rather disparaging comment on an article by Professor Charles Hartshorne. (124, n. 37) Though their doctrines are profoundly different, I think a concurrent reading of Duméry and Hartshorne on the problems of natural theology would be profitable. Each of them proposes an original solution to the perennial problem of theism. Perhaps Professor Hartshorne shares Duméry's fundamental concerns and taste for metaphysics as much as any other American philosopher. Thus it would be unfortunate if Duméry's phrase were to be the end of the dialogue. It is my hope that this translation will help to prolong and enlarge the conversation between French- and English-speaking philosophers.

The English translation of *The Two Sources of Morality and Religion*, Bergson's last great work and his most direct contribution to philosophy of religion, appeared almost exactly thirty years ago. The radically new philosophical situation that has developed since 1935 calls for another genial renewal of philosophy of religion. There is much reason to believe that with this little book Henry Duméry has inaugurated such a renewal. Thus it is an honor to add *The Problem of God* to the other important French contributions to the philosophical literature in English.

CHARLES COURTNEY

Paris
January 1964

A U T H O R ' S

Preface

WE COULD CONDUCT our inquiries on the category of the Absolute in several ways. We could take up again the traditional natural theologies and submit them to a critical examination. Or we could retrace the concrete history of Christian theism, that is, the representations that Christianity has generated and propagated within various cultures. Finally, we could study the structures of thought used by the believer when he implicitly affirms God in his religious behavior. But we have explained in an earlier work [1] why a completely different procedure is called for. Only one approach will be found here, and it has a rather novel character: we will attempt to see if the idea of God can withstand *critical dissolution*. By various means, we will attempt to *reduce* it in order to test its degree of coherence. If it comes out victorious from the discussion, the truth that it bears and the reality that it designates will have eluded the traps of language as well as those of the imagination.

1. Cf. *Critique et religion,* Conclusion. We refer to this work because, in fact and intention, our examination of the problem of God is closely dependent on it. We must refer as well to our two volumes of *Philosophie de la religion* which are the sequel of the present book.

The Problem of God

I / The God of Philosophers or the Living God?

GOD IS AFFIRMED first of all not by philosophical thought, but by spontaneous thought. Mankind had myths and religions very early, but metaphysics only much later. This is evidence that the needs of life, of psychology, and of society precede, and by a long time, methodical awareness of ideas and their ordering and classification. Criticism is always a fruit of maturity. There would be no consolation in seeing it born late if one did not know that, kept dependent on life and held in its wake, criticism is capable of participating in life's movement and profiting from its vigor. It would not be difficult to show that philosophy became sterile each time it separated itself from the living creations of the spirit in the sciences, the arts, or religion; or to show the contrary, that philosophy enriched itself each time it drew near to them. Through reflection on concrete contents, it has prospered; through abstraction or purely formal deduction, it has been endangered. This is a sufficient reason for asking it to maintain contact with the spiritual life in all its forms, especially its religious form. In the West, for example, it would be a sorry mistake to propose removing philosophy from the influence of Christianity. Moreover, faith and reason

[3]

having exchanged categories so much, it would be impossible to accept such a proposal.

One fact, however, is surprising: in the areas where faith and reason have been given separate domains, their conflicts become the most embittered. Instead of allowing them to get along as spontaneous thought and reflective thought, one seems to take pleasure in hardening them, opposing them to each other. It is thus that the great monotheistic idea has broken apart into two rival notions: the one remaining on the side of religion, the other limiting itself to the plane of abstraction. What is pejoratively called the *God of philosophers* has become the antithesis of the God of revelation, or at the very least its replica or noticeably impoverished double. By perpetuating this misunderstanding, we excite the spirit of polemicists in both camps. But it seems that this renders service neither to religion nor to philosophy. Perhaps Pascal had his reasons for humiliating the Cartesian God before that of Abraham, Isaac, and Jacob.[1] His eloquence must not keep us from realizing that the fault is shared by those who seize the notion of the Absolute for mysticism alone and those who confiscate it for rationalism alone.[2] In fact, the antinomy of the God of the learned and the God of the naive has its origins in a confusion concerning the responsibilities incumbent on the philosopher and the believer. It is advisable to reestablish the order of competencies in order to restore harmony and union.

1. Before Pascal, St. Augustine had used this formula, but he preferred that of Exodus 3, 14: *Ego sum qui sum.* Cf. *Sermon* VII, n. 7. Commented on in F. Cayré, *Dieu présent dans la vie de l'esprit* (Paris, 1951), p. 96.

2. "Neither scientism nor false mysticism," Maurice Blondel liked to say. (Cf. *La Pensée*, II, Paris, 1934, p. 135.)

[I] SPONTANEOUS THOUGHT
AND CRITICAL REFLECTION
RELIGIOUS THEISM AND PHILOSOPHICAL THEISM

THE PHILOSOPHER, first of all, must be aware that his discipline is only a reflective technique applied to lived experience. He does not supplant the concrete subject, the thinking and acting man. Only the latter is really engaged and brings values into play. Only he does a free act; only he effectively conforms the means at his disposal to the end he pursues. The philosopher is always dependent upon man and remains his pupil. He must clarify man, but not substitute himself for man. This is to say that philosophy always comes after life. Philosophy is a recovery of life, but it cannot be identified with life. Philosophy is, if you like, the word of life; it is not life itself.

By saying that philosophy is reflective, do we imply that human life is or can be reflective only because of philosophy? Here it is necessary to agree on the meaning of the words. Human life is conscious of itself; it is thought in act; it is light as well as liberty. Thus there is a word immanent to life, even before this word is raised to the level of philosophical discourse. In fact, man never acts without intentions; his practice is always directed by some theory. Hence spontaneous consciousness, or living and concrete spirituality, is mediated by ideas as well as by values. In this sense, man thinks and even reflects. But only in a very broad sense, for this reflection does not know itself as reflection; it remains tuned to the practical behavior that it guides and regulates. It holds to a straight course in the service of action; it is prospective, not retrospective. To become properly reflective, to be aware of itself as reflection, it must move to another plane, detach itself from the immediate, become both systematic and disinterested. If one prefers to call *reflection*, in the strict sense, this second act that returns to spontaneous thought in order to recover it methodically, he will contend that lived experience, even illuminated by the thought it carries, remains *non-reflected*, or, in the terminology of certain authors, *pre-reflective*. Thereby, even though life remains a thought in act, only philosophy will be called reflective. At last we see what relation is established between philosophy and life: the first is related to the second as the reflective to the spontaneous, knowledge to the concrete, judgment to being. There exist, consequently, two planes that must never be confounded: the *speculative plane* and the *concrete plane*. They are distinct, yet interdependent. Reflection lives on concrete life. For its part, the concrete would never become "reason" and system without a technically reflected ordering.

If the preceding is correct, the so-called *God of philosophers* risks being an illusion. The philosopher, having nothing other to do than criticize the products of spontaneous consciousness, is mistaken when he believes that he fabricates ideas, no matter which ones, and imagines that he gives them value. It is false that he invents them out of whole cloth; it is false that he endows them with value. He only recovers ideas and defines the condition under which the subject may acknowledge that they have value. The philosopher points out to the subject what responsibilities he must assume; but only the subject is capable of assuming them. The critical function does not take the place of the practical function; it uses the practical function and refers to it. But criticism neither eliminates nor dispenses with practice. These remarks have special value with respect to the idea of God and the scope proper to it. The philosopher *encounters* this idea; he is not the author of it.[3] He must therefore seek to know what it signifies and what role in life can be assigned to it. But he is not to mold it as he pleases nor turn it to uses which do not answer to the fundamental aspiration of the subject.

In these conditions, the God of philosophers is from the start a theft and a blunder. One pretends to believe that the idea of God is the property of philosophy, whereas it is borrowed from the religious life. One makes it the point of departure of a series of deductions, whereas it is a principle of conduct. One confiscates it for the benefit of so-called autonomous operations, whereas it is indiscretely smuggled in from spontaneous thought. How could it be surprising that the idea of God, so treated, becomes unrecognizable? One severs it from life and also would like it to return there: an untenable wager. The God of philosophers fails because of abstraction. He will never be more than a substitute product, an alibi for concrete theism. In life the God of philosophers or non-philosophers does not exist. There is only one God,[4] and the idea of him prompts definite actions; the idea and the actions are offered to critical reflection. We should not speak of a God peculiar to philosophers, but of a God that religion worships and that philosophy must take into consideration, as it does any other value.

3. The idea of God would indeed languish if it were sustained only by logical reasoning; on the other hand, it is vigorous when proclaimed by faith and instilled by worship. Practice serves it better than any dialectics.

4. At the very least, one sphere of the divine.

In any case, the affirmation of God is a work of free and spontaneous consciousness. The work of philosophical reflection is to state in what way this affirmation is coherent and obligatory, or on the contrary, vain and superfluous.

If there is no God of philosophers, neither is there a God of tradition who is inaccessible to reflection. Here the illusion does not come from the philosopher, but sometimes from the defender of religion.[5] The latter is correct in thinking that the affirmation of God rises

5. In a historical context where positive religion dreads naturalistic contaminations, above all in an academic setting where it is essential to distinguish truths of faith and truths of reason, there is opposition to the philosopher's taking for his own the notion of the living God, since he would thus appear to be arrogating the benefit of revelation to himself. Consequently, he either remains docile and appropriates for his natural theology only those elements which the theologian declares to be rational; or, taking as a pretext the poverty of the thought left to him, he sets revelation up as a principle and reduces God to an axiom. Rationalism is already germinally present in the mistaken segregation of religious and metaphysical evidences. If in actual fact the philosopher is not free to examine the idea of God as a function of the whole of human experience, including religious experience, he will set out from fragmentary initiatives and distorted evidence and will be able to discover only a mutilated or burlesqued notion of it. The apologist who would force him into such a situation is not entitled to reproach him with it later. Man's experience cannot be divided either *de facto* or *de jure*. It is easy to understand that one problematic should be employed to situate both that which calls attention to human powers and that which, on the other hand, proceeds from a special initiative of God. This problematic is indispensable to the theologian in one form or another, and, as method requires, the philosopher necessarily affirms its complement in his domain. Still, we should not conclude from this that the quest for God is not imposed on the philosopher as a function of the concrete life of man, of the *whole* man. Religion belongs to this concrete life. Thus, it cannot be left on the margin. It would be an exaggerated paradox to enjoin the philosopher to seek the idea of God wherever he sees fit, but to stipulate that he should steer clear of religion.

from spontaneous consciousness, especially in its religious form. But it is wrong for religion's advocate to confound the object of this affirmation with the modalities of the affirmation; it is wrong for him to believe that the transcendence of the divine mystery is extended to the materiality of the expressions that it takes on in human consciousness; with greater reason it is wrong for him to consider that his problematic is canonized by this transcendence. Some religious people seem to think that their logical instruments, and the frequently contestable manner in which they employ them, are rendered divine by the God they worship. This is as flagrant an abuse as that of the monopolistic philosopher who, shut up in his specialty, is ready to reduce the content of life to his own capacity for interpretation.[6] If the

6. Nothing is more strange than the reciprocal distrust of the philosopher and the believer (sometimes in the same individual). The former reproaches the latter for giving himself an extra dimension, for being "more than man." The latter reproaches the former for wishing to naturalize everything, including the divine. Each denounces a prejudice in the other. Many distinctions would be required to reconcile them; we will pursue the question elsewhere. But one thing can be said to the philosopher, and another to the believer. The philosopher who leaves religion aside, under the pretext that it is the affair of specially endowed minds and superhuman faculties, is not a rationalist. This abets the false mysticism which pretends that the means of expressing faith (I do not say faith itself) transcend humanity and belong to another world. Thus, the philosopher who regards religious experience and thought as taboo actually plays the fanatic. On the other side, the believer should not defend the object of his faith as if it were a meteor fallen from the sky. Even in the Christian religion, where the notion of revelation determines everything, it is necessary to discern an element of human construction. In these conditions, religion can be examined as a factual given, elaborated according to certain human procedures which can be grasped by criticism. Neither God nor grace is threatened by it. Alain, following Hegel, says that religions first of all are natural facts. We would agree with this, except to add that immanence is quite able to shelter a transcendence.

religious man judges God to be transcendent (a question that the philosopher in turn must ask himself), this is not to say that the representations he makes of this transcendence, and the procedures he employs to connect them, are essentially different from the modes of ordinary thought. Faith is undoubtedly a singular perspective on God, a unique intention. But when it formulates itself, its categories and schemes are taken from a logico-rational context upon which the philosopher has the right to bring a judgment. This is why, even if religious tradition has its own manner of posing God, the philosopher does not exceed his authority by demanding to verify this approach. In this sense, the God of tradition serves in no way as an antithesis to the supposed God of philosophers. Simply, he serves as spontaneous evidence for a critical attention that is concerned to study his content, to determine his meaning and scope. If there is an antithesis (not antinomy) anywhere, it is between the plane of lived theism and that of reflected theism. But this is not an antithesis between the God that is worshiped and the God that is demonstrated.

Thus the plane of religious theism is delivered up, in its entirety, to criticism. Is it not to be feared that it will be dissolved or absorbed by reflection? This fear is vain, if it is understood that reflection is tributary to life and that the latter remains, first and last, irreducible. Criticism begins from life and returns to life. It is only a reflective detour, the time of methodical judgment. It never suppresses that which nourishes it. Moreover, the philosopher will take care, in criticizing concrete theism,[7] to respect its specificity. Otherwise, he would be

7. By concrete theism, we refer more to the living intentionality that leads to the affirmation of God than to the academic

able neither to understand it nor to appreciate it at its proper value. To the extent that he nowhere confounds his role and that of the living subject, the plane of reflection and that of lived experience, it cannot be seen in what way he could mutilate the religious object. We acknowledge willingly that it is a delicate matter to treat the religious object, but we do not believe that it is impossible. For, by right, reflection is coextensive with the total range of human action. If it were otherwise, there would be no philosophy of religion. There would be no philosophy at all. Lived experience, whatever it is, is always "transcendent" to the reflective plane. In this respect religious reality is in the same position as all other "lived experience." It is more worthy of attention and respect only because it involves affirmations of greater consequence. In any case, it could evade criticism only by desiring to avoid reflection, and the result of this would not be an increase in nobility, but rather a lapse into intrigue.

We no more admit separatism in favor of religion than monopolism in favor of philosophy. The first is an activity of man; the second, an analysis of human initiatives, excepting none. The philosopher should not uproot the idea of God from the natural context where it germinates; nor should he monopolize it, pretend that he invented it, or manipulate it, as he would a formal concept empty of all spontaneous content. He should, from his point of view, reflect on it, criticize it, judge it; [8]

schemas about God. These schemas are as relative as any rational problematic. In contrast, the intentionality of which we speak coincides with the dynamism of the spirit and is as unchallengeable.

8. This situation is not unique to contemporary philosophy; it is found constantly in the history of doctrines. Plato and Plotinus, Augustine and Thomas Aquinas, Descartes and Spinoza, Male-

after which, if he considers it reasonable, that is, *affirmable* and practicable, he must put it back into the hands of the living subject, who will regulate his choice according to this instruction.[9] Thus, the problem of the God of philosophers will lead to no embarrassment at all; it will not even have taken shape as a problem. Its solution is found in realizing that it is an error to pose it.

On its side, the problem of the God of tradition will present no obstacle to criticism. For tradition is integral to life, and the latter lays itself open to reflection from beginning to end. There is then, properly speaking, neither the God of philosophers nor the God of tradition (in opposition to the former). There is *God*, affirmed by spontaneous consciousness (in its religious élan) and,

---

branche and Leibniz, Kant himself, Bergson and Blondel utilized and criticized the religious capital of their epochs. Christian writers sometimes call the thinkers of Antiquity the "pure philosophers." This is an equivocal manner of authorizing the Christian revelation. Theology itself admits that the idea of God is rational. But it has always germinated in a religious context before being taken up by the philosophers, including those of Antiquity. A. E. Taylor calls Plato "the creator of philosophical theism." (*Plato, The Man and his Work*, 4th ed., London, n.d., p. 493.) In fact, his role is limited to giving philosophical status to a religious idea.

9. This is said, obviously, of the subject capable of understanding the lesson given by the philosopher. In fact, religion remains the great educator of millions of minds. It succeeds in directing them by itself. It often does better than learned reflection because the skill proper to the latter is not conducive to the presentation of transpositions, or even approximate adaptations, of the true. Religion has the secret of satisfying the obscure regions of consciousness, those concerned with feeling and the practice of life in common. It captures unsuspected energies and orients them toward a spiritual ideal, of which it invents various representations ordered to the diverse levels of concrete subjectivity. It enlists the whole man; it engages all his powers.

by way of this affirmation, criticized by the philosopher. Philosophical theism is only concrete theism passed through the screen of criticism; [10] it is reflective appreciation of a spiritual act that is performed on the plane of effective engagement. Thus it is never a double of, or substitute for, lived theism. Philosophical theism is the methodical awareness and rigorous ordering of concrete theism. But only the subject relates himself to God, even after the philosopher has disclosed the valid conditions of this extremely intimate relationship. We do not imply that the philosopher's reflection does not maintain its independence or possess its own laws. The contrary is true. Philosophy has its own economy of a strictly rational order. Moreover, not being content to reflect what happens on the concrete plane, philosophy judges it. Philosophy not only describes; it *prescribes*. It demands that the subject conform to his decisions; otherwise, he may choose beyond the limits imposed by reflection, and thus choose badly. But ultimately, choice and concrete engagement revert to the subject. The philosopher limits himself to stating the rule for choice, the meaning and scope of engagement. Then it remains to choose, to act.

But how is this philosophical theism of which we speak to be elaborated? How does the critique of the idea of God proceed? The artifice of a construction out of

10. Moreover, religious theism mixes reflective elements with those of feeling. All, or very nearly all, religions have had sacerdotal castes to intellectualize the myths as well as to regulate the cult. Christianity itself arose in a cultural world where the old myths were already purified and partially rationalized. Because it subsequently developed in the environment of Greek metaphysics, its doctrine incorporated many philosophical notions. The result is that rational criticism finds in it an initial arrangement of categories. It is a question of profiting from this and pushing the effort of elucidation to completion.

whole cloth is denied to us. One does not shut himself up in his study to invent ideas; that would be a vain effort. The idea of God invades consciousness through education; it precedes inquiry. Far from being its product, it stimulates and harasses philosophical reflection. One can wish to confirm the idea of God, to enervate or dissolve it, but one does not create it. The only danger is to greet it with suspicion, or even with the prejudice of misunderstanding in order the better to reduce it. The first contact one makes with the idea of God determines the manner in which one will afterwards decide whether it is valuable or not. The first glance, the first regard, is never without importance. Everything is compromised at the outset if we have not decided to respect fully that which must be criticized in full. Thus certain precautions are necessary. When one approaches the idea of God and considers it without yet knowing its origin, it is unpardonable to ignore for long that religion is the context in which it blossoms most readily. To grasp it, examine and judge it, without checking where and how it shows what it is capable of, can only be a defect in method. We do not require an endless investigation by the philosopher, or a decision in favor of Christianity, still less an act of faith, this being of a different order. We do demand that he know where he starts from, that he be aware of the extent, or the limits, that he assigns to his initial experience and investigation. If we hold that, for better or for worse, Christianity is part of the situation of the contemporary thinker in the heart of Western civilization, it is because it is an historical fact. It is also because Christianity has received its structures from the West and because each of us is able to find in it something of our type of thought or style of life. In any case, if one were to examine the idea of God by imagining that he fabricates it, or by exploiting it in an arbitrary fashion, or by neglecting to put it back into the complexity of the religious given in which it germinates and bears fruit, he would deprive himself of the best information about it. He would discover only a pale replica of this idea, not the idea itself with the vividness proper to it.

Religion provides the statement of the difficulty to be resolved. For it furnishes, more or less elaborated, the *category* of the Absolute, which accompanies the *scheme* of transcendence. The necessary clarifications on the notions of category and scheme will be found in our book, *Critique et religion,* a study of method. Let us recall only that recourse to these words does not imply that we subscribe to Kantianism, especially its formalism and transcendental idealism. The example of religion, where form and content are mutually conditioning, is sufficient evidence to warrant the rejection of all disjunction between them. The notion of "form" or "structure," in the sense of the phenomenologists, is much nearer to the religious reality which always associates the objective and the subjective. If these reservations are made, the terms "category" and "scheme" are very useful for designating, on the one hand, the fundamental concepts, and on the other hand, the imaginative structures in which the idea is incarnated.

Here criticism comes to grips with the notion of the Absolute, accompanied by its scheme. How is it to be accepted, purified, integrated? That is the question. From this perspective, we quickly grasp what services Christianity renders to philosophy. However, that is only of secondary interest. Our attention must bear essentially on the philosophical attempt to subject the data of religion to an examination. In accordance with good method, we will examine the latter only with a view toward establishing what indices of truth are to be credited to the realities it presents. We are interested in the inner coherence of religion's principal representations; we are particularly interested in the rigor the idea of God or the category of the Absolute possesses, and in the value of the scheme of transcendence. In this inquiry we will be led to put the perspectives of history and criticism in concert, because religion, like all human activity, is both a given and a signification, the history of a genesis and the foundation of an *eidetic*. But that which is associated is not necessarily confounded. This back-and-forth movement between history and reflection ultimately will be to the profit not of curiosity but of judgment.

Now the category and the scheme of the notion of the Absolute are able, it seems, to give rise to three series of considerations. The first concerns the approach by which God can be affirmed; the second touches on the nature of God, as well as on the nature of the mind which is in contact with him; the third has reference to the essence of religion or living spirituality, inasmuch as God appears there in a certain type of relation. Thus natural theology, philosophy of mind, and phenomenology of religion are at stake in this debate. This convenient division, however, reveals its artificiality. For the relation of man to God must be presented as an indivisible whole; otherwise it appears illusory. Thus, let us not be duped by a clever arrangement; it is suitable for exposition, but it must never mask the unity of the problem.

[II] THE PROBLEM OF THE EXISTENCE OF GOD
AND THE PROBLEM OF HIS NATURE

THE RELIGIOUS SOUL comes to God through faith, hardly at all through dialectic. This is not to say that the man of faith does not have recourse to numerous and subtle reasonings if ever he attempts to think his faith. But faith itself lies none the less on a plane more profound than any reflection. Thus we can say that it belongs to a separate order. The act of believing in God is a *sui generis* venture; to study it as such, it would be necessary to make a general critique of faith. We will be occupied with that in other works; the present chapter has another object.[11] It is simply to state what happens when the idea of God, incorporated into belief, falls under the regard of philosophy.

On this very point, observation discloses an almost constant procedure that is extremely revealing. It seems that philosophy's only task concerning God is to *prove* his existence, which is peremptorily affirmed by faith. Reason is asked to establish by its methods, what religion achieves, at less expense, on its own. Everything happens as if faith, which has its own certitude, had need either of being reinforced by reasoning (which is not at all specifically religious) or of being persuaded that it sustains infinitely more than reason (and this is

11. The reason our study of concrete theism does not lead to a critical exposition of the notion of *religious faith* is that it is impossible to define faith critically inasmuch as the principal objects on which it bears cannot be examined.

not of much profit to the latter). In both cases, there is something strange about the process.

Certainly it can be understood that faith, since it penetrates the totality of consciousness, involves a rational plane. Belief in God presupposes, in this respect, reason's adhesion to the idea of God and the equally reasonable conviction of his existence. For most Christian philosophers, the possibility of a rational discourse on God is founded on this point. Natural theology exposes the rational elements integral to belief. It organizes and appraises them, although differently than faith does. However, even that procedure is not without some drawbacks.

In the first place, this process of bringing to light the rational elements included in belief seems legitimate only if it remains subordinate to faith. Using the medieval formula, we can say that it remains meaningful for those who put philosophy in the service of theology. If the philosophical demonstration of the existence of God could not be taken up and transcended by belief in God, it would be manifestly impossible to bring the affirmation of reason in accord with the affirmation of faith. The moment one seeks, in the name of reason, to undermine the foundations of belief, natural theology becomes the operation of bringing into focus that element of belief which permits it to lay claim to rational proofs.[12] Methodological considerations make it clear, however, that this procedure is acceptable only to someone who previously admits two things: first, the division, into two sectors, of truths of faith and truths of reason; second, a philosophical au-

12. In this sense, natural theology is apologetics. By turning their objections back on them, it prevents unbelievers from advancing a prejudiced rejection.

tonomy circumscribed within the limits of the exigencies of dogmatics. Those who, to the contrary, refuse
all dualism (or even the risk of it) between faith and reason, as well as any attempt to limit philosophical inquiry
to a restricted area of truths,[13] can only advocate recourse to other approaches.

There is another more serious disadvantage to enclosing natural theology in the frame we just described.
If one holds that intimacy with God is achieved only
through faith, whereas God's existence falls within the
scope of demonstration, he becomes the victim of a
logical device. He projects on God a distinction of
perspectives that was conceived [14] only in order to
maintain two sources of truths, the one transcendent
and the other immanent; in return, it is forgotten that
the "transcendent" truths come to expression within
immanence. But how is God able to divide himself into
the God of faith and the God of reason? How can he
become simultaneously, or by turns, the locus of mystery
and the object of demonstration? One of two things
must be chosen: either he is mystery and no explanation
of it can be produced; or he is object and explanation
triumphs over, but also dissolves, mystery. However,
does this not confound two orders of questions, one
concerned with what God is, the other with the fact that
he is? It can be answered that if it is important not to
confuse these questions, it is also important not to
separate them. Now they are inevitably separated when
they are related to processes as different as those of
spiritual freedom in the order of belief and those of

13. Cf. *Critique et religion*, chap. III.
14. Perhaps this distinction was made primarily for academic
convenience, so as to classify theology and philosophy according
to different objects.

intelligible necessity in the logical order. Faith does not
sever them; hypothetically, faith is assured of revelation
concerning both the nature and the existence of God. As
for reason, how could it establish the existence of a
being if it were ignorant of the conditions under which
it is able to be, if it is? It is easily understood that a
theologian seeks to found in reason the existence of a
God whose prerogatives he knows through faith. For
him natural theology amounts to finding an argument
that refutes the principal denials of the unbeliever; that
is a useful tactic and it is impressive. But the philosopher finds himself in a completely different situation.
He raises simultaneously the questions of the *quid* and
the *quod,* of the nature of God and his existence; he
considers the two questions to be indissoluble.[15] Thus
the philosopher, if he poses the question of God, will
acknowledge the right of posing it only with respect to
God's existence or non-existence, that is, his mystery.
He will not say that God exists, as an object exists, nor
that he is this or that, as an object is this or that. In a
word, the question of the existence of God and the
connected question of his nature are carried beyond the
plane where their disjunction renders the first soluble by
simple objective explanation and the second soluble by
the fixed determinations of faith (it being forgotten that
their character as determinations necessarily refers to a

15. Brunschvicg is right in saying that the manner of
establishing the proofs of the existence of God is dependent on
the idea one has of his nature. "Not only the modality of the
proofs that we will endeavor to establish in favor of his existence,
but also their legitimacy, are dependent on the idea, more or less
pure and intellectual, more or less true, that one has of him." (*De
la vraie et de la fausse conversion,* Paris, 1951, p. 123.) In the
language of criticism, the value of God is the value of the mind
that conceives him. Each one has the God he deserves.

discursive power of reason). That shows why criticism cannot ratify a system of representations that leads to thinking of God as divided within himself,[16] his depths being confided to faith, his existence offered separately to philosophical demonstration.

Moreover, the dualistic systems become tangled in their own problematic. On the metaphysical plane they hold that in God essence and existence are one, and on the methodological plane, that his existence is demonstrable without his essence being clarified by reason. This inconsistency is aggravated by another, typical of the same systems: that of first establishing the existence of God and then launching forthwith a determination of his essence, without saying how the passage from existence to essence is able to follow upon their initial disjunction. Then comes a third contradiction that attempts to make up for the other two: since it is important to limit the determination of essence, for fear of crossing the threshold of mystery, one divides, if we may say so, the divine essence into two parts, one penetrable by reason, the other reserved to faith. If one retraces these three procedures—disjunction, then reunion of essence and existence, and finally division (at the second degree) of essence—they will be recognized as artificial schemes that are tainted with spatiality: the scheme of extra-position, the scheme of juxtaposition, the scheme of superposition (supernature).[17] Is a natural theology, developed in terms of these schemes, anything other than a logical contrivance?

16. This is to treat God as a thing or a solid, as an object in space.

17. We will see how the positive aspect of the scheme of supernature can be preserved. *Cf. Philosophie de la religion* (Paris, 1957).

This is why we prefer another manner of resolving the difficulty. Can the same object be known and believed at the same time and in the same respect? St. Thomas answers no, St. Bonaventure answers yes.[18] Undoubtedly this opposition would be transcended if it were held that the line of demarcation passes, not between faith and reason,[19] but rather between *living spirituality* and *critical reflection*.

With this we are approaching the solution: it consists in saying that belief is entirely on the side of the concrete subject, whereas knowledge belongs to criticism. But both belief and knowledge have to do with the same reality, the God of living spirituality.[20] The phantom of a notional Absolute is not reintroduced on the reflective plane. From the start, the reflective plane re-

18. Texts cited and discussed in E. Gilson, *La philosophie de saint Bonaventure,* 2nd ed. (Paris, 1943), p. 91, and *Le Thomisme,* 4th ed. (Paris, 1942), p. 29. [English translation by L. K. Shook, C.S.B., *The Christian Philosophy of St. Thomas Aquinas* (New York, 1956), p. 17.] St. Bonaventure holds that if it is a question of an object transcendent to human thought, it is necessary to know it and believe it at the same time. Because knowledge and belief together are not too much for thinking an object which transcends each of them singly, they must associate their efforts, and even admit that man *in via* is not able to perceive the divine mystery in its true light. On the contrary, St. Thomas holds that when knowledge decides on the basis of first principles, faith should not intervene.

19. We do not say that faith and reason are not distinct; we affirm and repeat that they are. But it is still necessary to understand what distinguishes them. To be content with a mutual compatibility—faith-reason (or theology-philosophy)—is insufficient; faith, in order to express itself, borrows from philosophy. Furthermore, this dualism leads to disguising God in the masks of *God of reason* and *God of religion*. And thus one returns to the false problem of the God of philosophers and the God of simple believers.

20. Knowledge thereby directly sanctions mystery and yet maintains its character of rational criticism.

fers to the living Absolute, as reflection refers to the plane of lived realities. The reflective plane defines the conditions under which the free subject can hold that God exists and under which he can serve him religiously. We no longer need to pose the problem of the relationship between a *knowing* and a *believing* which divide up, so to speak, the reality of God. Knowledge deals with the whole extent of belief, of which it formulates the *a priori* conditions. In other words, criticism no longer has to affirm that God exists, while leaving intimate communication with him to the subject. It simply states what is demanded of the subject in order that he, without betraying the imperative of reflection, can acknowledge the Absolute in his existence and in his mystery. It is no use proving that God exists if we do not indicate at the same time the necessary value he has for man. Indeed, the problem of his being and that of his value are one. This is to say that criticism must achieve knowledge of belief rather than of an object that is excised from a belief, then dealt with on its margin. Otherwise, one inevitably reverts to a God of philosophy which is not that of religion. This difficulty is overcome if critical reflection limits itself to recovering the affirmation of living spirituality in order to disclose its meaning and its norms.

Does this point of view make natural theology less reliable? Does it weaken the classical arguments? We will see that it does just the opposite. It does not burden faith with the worry of proving that God exists, as if reason were incapable of taking a position on this matter. By giving criticism the mission of verifying all the affirmations of practice, we do not encourage fideism; we elevate reflection, giving it universal jurisdiction. It remains true for us that reason has the capacity to prove

God,[21] and in a more complete sense than is ordinarily granted to it. For the judgment it will produce on the reflective plane is a *categorical* summons, addressed to the subject, to come to a decision. But in doing this, reflection will not pronounce in favor of an Absolute situated on its plane; it will refer to the only Absolute worthy of the name, that which the subject can discern in his mind and obey in his conduct. In fact, philosophy's task is less to prove God than to establish the subject in the rational and moral dispositions through which the notion of the Absolute will prove itself. Or, if philosophy is able to construct the proof of God, it is because God is, from the beginning, immanent to the reason and to all the powers of the concrete subject. Criticism only transposes and makes rigorous a norm that *remains implicit* but *is really operative in all consciousness.*[22]

Thus, the sole duty of the philosopher is to examine

21. We will see how.

22. Unfortunately, the role of philosophy is not always understood in this fashion. It is confused with thought in act, with the reason or reflection of the concrete subject, although it is only the technically ordered awareness of it. Blondel put it well: "reasonable reason underlies rational reason." (*La Pensée*, I, Paris, 1934, p. 178.) This leads to innumerable verbal misunderstandings. If we say, from our point of view, that the task of philosophy is neither to invent the idea of God nor to construct arguments in the void, some will understand that we are dispossessing reason of its rights or even that we leave it to mysticism to be occupied with God. We hold, on the contrary, that philosophy is nothing other than reason, but reason become fully conscious of itself, master of its criteria; it borrows ideas and values from living consciousness (thought in act), then it systematizes and judges them. In this respect its intervention is decisive. Without the *moment* of philosophical reflection, spirituality would remain as spontaneous activity. God would be lived but not truly thought. In order to reach the critical plane, theism must, like every spontaneous movement, pass from the plane of life to that of reflection. This expresses the indispensable role that we give to philosophy in natural theology.

the meaning and value that the idea of God bears for living spirituality. He converges on an actually lived intention, without having to take the place of the concrete subject and pursue it himself. If, on the contrary, the philosopher severs the critical function from the content of life, if he isolates it, if he sets it up as a self-sufficient system, the notion of God will become for him something quite different from what it is for spontaneous consciousness. It will take on the characteristics of the *God of philosophers;* in other words, its own face will be hidden by this mask. Certainly it is understandable that the professional philosophers abstract from the positivity and particularity of the religious traditions; knowledge of these traditions is only one specialized branch of philosophical criticism. But it is incomprehensible that a philosopher would study the idea of the Absolute without referring to spiritual experience, that is, to the process of conversion that initiates, independently of cultual determinations, the religious attitude in general.[23] If he fails to proceed in this way, it is hard to see what could support him. The prejudice of relating essences, disconnected from their attachment in reality, is not a satisfactory foundation; rather, it is the refusal of the only normal and legitimate foundation. Consequently, if the philosopher ends up with an abstract God, a God-axiom, a God-law, or even worse, a God-thing, he has only himself to blame. No one has

23. All religions suppose a movement of inner conversion (the scope varies according to the requirements of the given religion). A similar process, by which consciousness attempts to rejoin the Absolute or the divine, develops beneath, or rather in the heart of, the structural ensembles. This process, this effective advance, is the concern of "reflection"; the philosopher must determine its meaning, control its orientation, and test its value.

ever worshiped such a God, for he hardly transcends the cunning of the one who constructs him. He is not even raised to the level of the living spirit, inasmuch as it is creative subjectivity; he is confounded with a product of thought, with an object that one attempts to circumscribe. Far from being an Absolute, he is a determination—the highest perhaps, but posed in a manner similar to the others. He is found in the prolongation of no real aspiration, of no sincere adherence; he is simply conceived as an intellectual opinion, as a logical possibility and, in the extreme case, as a fiction.

Just a little attention to the meaning of the concrete will show that this result is deceptive. The most astonishing thing is not that this capacity for distraction is found in thinkers of only slight religious temperament. The greatest scandal is that religious minds believe it is necessary to transpose the problem of God onto the plane of a criticism without interiority. This concession to formalism becomes a betrayal. Once engaged in a purely notional matrix, it is only a matter of evoking the adventure of the idea of God. Under the pretext of rational selection, of demonstrative proof, one lapses into a veritable thing-ism.

[III] CRITICISM OF ANY NOTIONAL OR EXPLANATORY "ABSOLUTE"

WHEN THE PHILOSOPHER cuts himself off from concrete theism, he desires to reach God at the end of an analytic regression. He strives to follow point by point the series of finite causes in order to discover finally one last link that will assure the solidity of the entire chain. This reasoning is simple, facile, classic. But it is not sufficient that it has become an old habit, an academic exercise. That does not guarantee its universal validity. What is, in fact, the true logical nature of this reasoning? It belongs to the order of objective explanation. It is able to, and actually does, work wonders in the domain of scientific experimentation.[24] This will to analyze, this concern for ordered regression, and this effort to go back to the first principle are all respectable. But the question is whether they are legitimate when applied to God; likewise, whether their postulates do not render them inoperative outside a certain sphere.

Can God be the final term of a continuous series? That is the whole question. Would not being made part of a homogeneous series mark his downfall? Religion protests here, but it is not alone; the spiritual exigency refuses to contradict its own meaning by *objectifying* or *reifying* the category of the Absolute. God, inserted in an objective series, or placed at the summit of one, is enclosed in its orbit; he is *in series* with the other terms. In short, he is compromised with the relative. Let us note that the scheme of transcendence is not able to serve here as a corrective. Its use in such a context would withdraw God too late from the objective enterprise which had been considered necessary to establish his existence. When one has begun with objectivism, it is necessary to finish with it. But in finishing with it,

24. Did not Kant's error lie in wishing to adopt a method in philosophy analogous to that of physics? Cf. *Critique de la raison pure*, preface to 2nd ed., trans. Barni-Archambault, I, p. 22, note 1: "This method, borrowed from the physicist . . ." [English translation by Norman Kemp Smith, *Immanuel Kant's Critique of Pure Reason* (London, 1933), p. 23 n.a.] At least Kant was careful to avoid using this method to resolve the problem of God. He even went so far as to prove that with such a method all demonstration of God is impossible.

one conceives the Absolute as object and forfeits the right of affirming him as mystery.

The very postulates of the objectivist method are a reason for mistrusting it. How can reasoning be made to bear on sense experience, or on internal (psychological) experience, so as to demonstrate both: 1) the incapacity of the creature to explain himself through himself; 2) the capacity of the creature to pose the Absolute as his explanation? Either the point of departure and the point of arrival are homogeneous, in which case the conclusion is rigorous but the second term is absorbed into the first (ruining the notion of God); or the point of departure and the point of arrival are heterogeneous, in which case the Absolute is safe but the consequence unfounded (ruining reasoning). The attempt to hold the relative and the absolute in the same logical dimension has failed.

Moreover, it is rather surprising that the creature who attempts to justify himself finds his explanation in an other, solely because he does not find it in himself. It can always be objected that there is a third solution, i.e., that the creature has no explanation. Furthermore, if the creature poses God as his explanation, this "explanation" must be inscribed in him as an integral part of his own immanence; it is surprising then that at the moment of self analysis the creature does not find it in himself. If the explanation could be found, there would be no need to search for it outside. In any case, if God were only the explanation of the creature, he would be his explanatory principle, his immanent cause; it cannot be seen in what way God would be transcendent to him. Moreover, the statement that the creature searches for a truly transcendent cause because only that which exists of itself is able to sustain that which does not exist of itself is not a proof, but an expression of the postulate that not to exist of itself is necessarily equivalent to existing through an other. Now that is indemonstrable. Or rather, it is verifiable only for the case in which he who does not exist of himself carries an energy that both discloses his determinations to him and surpasses them, indeed exceeds them and outdistances them each time they appear. This energy then becomes the sign that there is in man, beyond the determinations, a transdetermination in act whose implications must be sought. But formal reasoning does not take this route. Perhaps it takes this route unknowingly; one can only wish for its good that it would. In any case, it does not acknowledge that it does; on the contrary, it endeavors to support itself directly with explanation of the inferior term by the superior, the former held to be unexplainable at its level. One immediately falls back into the circle we described earlier: either the superior is of a kind with the inferior, and then the tautology is flagrant; or they are of different kinds, and in this case heterogeneity breaks the explanatory chain. In each case the argument is ruined. We can all the more freely register our disbelief that the Christian systems of the past surrendered completely to the objectivist temptation.[25]

Nevertheless, this temptation is not unreal. It holds for a general climate, a frame of mind. It results from certain technical needs of the philosopher and from the facticious opposition that several authors institute between *the philosophical mind* and *the religious mind*. The philosopher, it is often said, seeks God as the

25. We will try to show this in the following chapter.

ultimate principle, the highest explanation; [26] the religious man seeks him as the principle of life and salvation. This amounts to saying that the mission of the philosopher is to explain everything but to understand nothing, whether in existence or in the concrete inquiry into values. For if the ultimate purpose of philosophical reflection is to make deductions at the margin of real life, if it is interested in something other than the conditions of salvation, it can be a new algebra, but it will no longer be either knowledge of self or an approach to wisdom. Fortunately, on principle and in fact, philosophy does not succeed in being only a combination of unfounded ideas. Whether the philosopher is aware of it or not, the notions he connects hold together by means of the living Cogito, and the latter, instead of being a pure form, is an act which expresses itself at different levels.[27] Consequently, philosophy remains the restoration, or the methodical recovery, of an act that transcends its multiple expressions. Philosophy mediatizes this act, it depends on it, it returns to it; it is able neither to supplant it nor to immerse it in an objective series. This is why the philosopher is justified in working for the unification of consciousness, but not for its suppression as act. If he elaborates a system, it must be a system of the conditions of the realization of this act, not one of explanatory synthesis that would permit consciousness to disappear in the contemplation

26. Cournot, for example, considers the idea of the Absolute to be "the supreme reason of all things." (*Traité de l'enchaînement des idées fondamentales dans les sciences et dans l'histoire*, par. 518.) But it is precisely Cournot who feels the need to have recourse to a trans-rationalism in order to save a place for the supernatural.

27. In our *Philosophie de la religion*, the theory of the act-law justifies this point of view.

of its elements. For these elements are only expressions of the act, not the act itself. The act remains irreducible; by essence it is non-objectifiable. It is necessary then to abandon the attempt to make philosophy an abstract system; it does not systematize, it only unifies the living spirit. In this respect it remains, with full justification, philosophy of salvation, criticism of life, knowledge of the practical. It is not opposed to religion as a rival or competitor. Philosophy simply procures for religion the means of a *recovery* of the latter's categories and schemes, the advantage of a reflection on itself, that the religious man does not attempt and is not able to attempt at the level of his behavior.

That the spiritual act cannot be reduced we have had occasion to note in another study.[28] To be convinced of this we need only to recall its essentially inventive character, its capacity for indefinitely re-editing the same operations, as well as its constant presence to self while in action.[29] Fecundity, universality, and self-regulation protect the spiritual act definitively from all "reification"; it can be neither exhausted nor limited nor saturated by forms or laws. Since it is impossible to bar the spiritual act from life and efficacy, it remains to take hold of its products in order to dominate them. But when the latter become determined, fixed, and objectified, they are only witnesses of the spirit's past action, vestiges of its creation. And even in this case there is nothing to prevent the subject from not recognizing himself in what he has done; he retains the freedom either to undo or do it again or recover it in order to make a new use of it. Certainly the irreversibility of

28. Cf. *Critique et religion,* chap. II.
29. It is known that throughout his writings Pierre Lachièze-Rey stressed these various points.

time seems to work against the subject: that which has been accomplished remains so forever. But the subject retains the means of recapturing and reorienting what he has done. The past does not rise up again, but it can be either re-willed or taken up by a renovating will which integrates it into an original project. Thus the spiritual act, barring a culpable abdication, is always able to escape from its past action in order to continue acting.

If the act escapes each attempt at reduction, it is vain to try to display it on an objective plane. Likewise, if it is thought that the idea of God, or rather God himself (because the Absolute, we shall see, is not held in a determination),[30] is the goal of a lived intention, of a concrete aspiration (phenomenological experience is already a witness of it), there can be no question of enclosing him in the objective register.[31] Far from

30. Commenting on Malebranche, Lucien Labbas writes, "If we do not talk of the idea of God it is because there is no idea of God. . . . There is no idea of the infinite being that represents it and in relation to which it could be asked whether it exists or not." (*La grâce et la liberté chez Malebranche*, Paris, 1931, p. 9.) For his part, Henri Gouhier analyzes the reasons why there is not, strictly speaking, an idea of God in Malebranche's doctrine; cf. *La philosophie de Malebranche et son expérience religieuse*, (Paris, 1926), pp. 329 ff. There is, as well, the famous formula of Gabriel Marcel: ". . . when we speak of God it is not of God that we are speaking." (*Journal métaphysique*, Paris, 1935, 11th ed. p. 258.) [English translation by Bernard Wall, *Metaphysical Journal* (London, 1952), p. 266.] Marcel later returned to this formula in order to refine it; cf. Michel Bernard, Appendix to *La philosophie religieuse de Gabriel Marcel, Étude critique* (Paris, 1952), p. 144.

31. It is known how K. Jaspers struggles against any attempt to objectify God. "God does not allow himself to be grasped as a worldly thing." (*Introduction à la philosophie*, trans. J. Hersch, Paris, 1950, p. 58.) [English translation by Ralph Manheim, *Way to Wisdom* (New Haven, 1954), p. 46.] "I am sure that God is, through the same decision that makes me exist. This certitude

making him a link, even the highest one, in an explanatory chain, he must be considered not as that which is explained or as that which explains, but as that which refuses to enter into the domain of explanation. In the order of explanation, cause and effect must be of the same type. Now, between an explanatory series and the Absolute, there is the infinite distance from the reflective to the concrete, an impassable distance for any other initiative than that of the acting subject. God remains on the side of life, while objectivist thought would like to place him on the side of determinations. Certainly a critique must be undertaken of this approach that leads to God, but the approach is not to be absorbed in the critique itself, to the point of confounding the plane on which reflective technique moves with that of concrete subjectivity.

When a philosophical system attempts to integrate the Absolute in order to round itself off in its own formal unity, there can be no mistake about it: what it integrates is not the Absolute but a determination complementary to those already posed. It is known how every determination calls forth its opposite, assumes it by transforming itself in order to give a richer determination that becomes in turn the point of departure of a new antithesis for a new synthesis. Now the moment occurs when this dialectical play reveals itself to be endless. There is a temptation to limit it by imagining a synthesis that recapitulates all the others, goes beyond them and balances them. The notion of the Absolute is often used to this end; it stops the movement by justifying it. But this manner of

does not permit shutting God up in a formula, but makes of him a presence for existence." (*Ibid.*, p. 56.) [English translation, p. 45.] However, Jaspers' context is different from ours.

stopping the movement implies one of two things: either the Absolute is the supreme idea which retains the same essence as the inferior ideas, and then the brake is not efficacious, for each idea is relationship to others and the movement is started again; or the Absolute is more than an idea, more than what is thought in a determinate category (of the object or of the subject), and in this case he completely transcends the plane on which, hypothetically, the system develops.[32] Either alternative fails to render credible a transcendence of the subject-object correlation situated at the same level as the deductive chain. In fact, we will see

32. Hegel rightly conceived an Absolute in which being and meaning are reconciled. But not, however, without equivocation. For this Absolute is realized only by way of human consciousness. One wonders, then, who exercises the determining power. Either it is man, and in this case it is a question of an anthropology applied to the Absolute. Or it is the suprahuman Logos, and in this case the Logos must not be confounded with human history; expressing itself in it, it must remain meta-historical and, as well, transcategorical. "The chief difficulty with Hegelianism," writes Jean Hyppolite, "is the relation of the *Phenomenology* to the *Logic*, we would say today of anthropology to ontology. The one studies human reflection proper, the other the absolute reflection that passes through man. Hegel believed that in the *Phenomenology* he was able to understand human reflection in the light of absolute knowledge (the for-us of this work), and it seems to us that Hegelian ontology contains the principle of this comprehension. He also believed he could manifest the becoming-knowing-absolute of the human consciousness, as if this becoming were a history. History is indeed the place of this passage, but this passage is not itself an historical fact." (*Logique et existence*, Paris, 1953, p. 247.) For our part, we will attempt to escape the Hegelian antinomy: 1) by placing the logos at once in and above its empirical expressions; 2) by distinguishing it from the Absolute, for the latter is not to be subject to the law of expression, which involves the multiplicity of determinations. This distinction will permit us to declare that the logos is *human* (although meta-psychological), instead of confounding it with the Absolute. These precisions are made in our work, *Philosophie de la religion*, Part One.

that such a transcendence can be obtained only through the apperception of a radical productivity, which in no way resembles a finished system or a perfect outline fully realized. It is useless to pose God as the summit or as the end of an objective series. In those contexts he is either distorted or inassimilable. He resists the reduction that one desires to make of him; he does not allow himself to be reduced to an ultimate idea (which, moreover, is meaningless since each idea is related and not the end of a series).

Still, this failure is instructive. Perhaps certain philosophers are so ready to attempt to use God as a stopgap for their dialectic because they are ignorant of its true limits. They imagine that by constructing a system of ideas they have found an absolute order, the order of essences just as it is in God. Convinced that they are working to restore the divine order, they think that the formal rigor of this order is guaranteed by God himself. Consequently, after having displayed their chains of reasons, which they readily believe are as complex as the order of things, they conclude that there is nothing more to do than name the true author of this dialectic: God. The system is thus complete; it takes account of the arrangement of the world and of he who created it. But precisely the whole question is to know whether God can be identified with a subject of determinations. Nothing is less certain. If one wishes, God can be made a wisely ordering demiurge, a subtly calculating mathematician, even a creator who brings about the act of the possibles he harbors in his essence. But all these metaphors remain anthropomorphic. They consist in attributing to God our logical patterns, our scientific methods, our own capacities. This order of essences discovered by us is in reality an ordering that proceeds from our knowledge and aptitudes. It is a multiplicity more or less overcome, an analysis more or less well executed. At bottom, it is our product. Projecting it onto God requires considerable audacity, for such a "projection" amounts to crediting the Absolute with the incertitude of our apprehensions of the world. Certainly these give us the possibility of acting on things; better, they permit us to realize ourselves. Thus they have their utility and even their truth, both attested by the service they render. But to place them in the divine essence it is necessary first of all to decree that the divine is in our image, and this assertion is not without difficulties.[33] To project onto God the constellation of our ideas or our values is to wish to make him assume the responsibility for our systems. At the extreme, it is to identify God with the sum of our constructions. After that is done, he serves to guarantee our affirmations or our action. There is God: guardian of our laws, place of our ideas, point of attachment for our truths; he founds security, gives us a clear conscience, and exempts us from a long effort of inquiry.

This God-refuge, this God who ratifies our conventions because he carries them in himself, this God who consecrates our values because they are inscribed in our essence is, alas, only human nature, if we pretend to forget its relativity and ambiguity. The need for an absolute explanation reveals here its true significance:

33. Feuerbach asks, "Is the knowledge that man has of God the knowledge that God has of himself? What a dichotomy and what a contradiction. Turn the sentence around and you have the truth. The knowledge that man has of God is the knowledge that man has of himself, of his own essence." (*Das Wesen des Christentums*, p. xxiv; cited in H. Niel, *De la médiation dans la philosophie de Hegel*, Paris, 1945, p. 351, note 71.) [English translation by George Eliot, *The Essence of Christianity* (New York, 1957), p. 230.]

it shows that man finds the responsibility for his
creations too heavy. He hastens to lay it down and
entrust it to a being who would work with man's powers
without having his weaknesses. He forgoes inventing
his own salvation, preferring to adhere to fully developed values located in the Absolute and provided with
an immutable foundation. Man's freedom henceforth
has nothing to create; it has only to follow the order that
is marked out for it from on high. In sum, under the
pretext of submissiveness to God, man ends up by
considering as definitive and fully sufficient the system
fabricated, with assumptions held unconsciously, by
himself. Theism consists then in no longer knowing
that one is the author of his own ideas.

Thus, recourse to God with a view to stabilizing a
dialectic is only a ruse to justify it. The crucial step here
is to realize that God neither relies on our determinations
nor shoulders them. Explanatory thought requires him
to do both. This is its error. Whoever wants to protect
himself from it must draw the conclusion of this
argument and courageously envisage a human creativity
of determinations. The philosopher will discover that
God is not the final explanation, because all explanation,
and to begin with, all determination, goes only from
man to man. Are we thereby thrown back to a radical
relativism? That is no longer a closed question. Determinations imply the determining subject, as reflection
supposes the spiritual act. Now it is possible that this act
refers to something other than itself, to a principle. This
would no longer be a principle of explanation, but a
principle of self-position, a principle which is a source
not of determination, but of transdetermination. But let
us not anticipate. It suffices to note that the refusal of
explanatory theism is not necessarily the refusal of all

theism. Rather, by eliminating false absolutes we prepare ourselves for the discovery of the living God. It would be mockery to qualify as philosophical the theism that takes the Absolute to be the result of abstract investigations. For philosophy, we have said, by virtue of its critical function, refers first of all to the spiritual act and seeks to understand what it wants in order to lead it whither it tends.

II / Demonstration
or "Reduction"?

How CAN WE TREAT the idea of God without lapsing into objectivism? Is there a means of providing valid arguments in its favor without measuring it by a standard suitable for things? Yes or no—after so much beating about the bush, can the existence of God be proved, and is it possible to search for what his nature is or is not? Certainly there is a means; it is suggested, we believe, by religion or living spirituality, whose witness the philosopher must criticize. By retracing the spiritual movement which, in fact, leads to God for all those who endeavor to discern his presence, one can bring to light certain secret incentives, certain intentions whose efficacy is indubitable. It is this movement, this process of conversion, that we are going to describe. It is situated less in the order of notions than in that of motions, less on the plane of concepts than on that of values. Even if we speak a technical language, it will be understood that we refer to attitudes and initiatives of the naive as well as the wise.

[1] REDUCTION DISCOVERS THE ONE

THE PROCEDURE WE WANT to develop is not at all original. Husserl named it "reduction"; we will call it that ourselves.[1] It could as well be called *apperception*, a word borrowed freely from Leibniz. If we use these terms, it is not in order to innovate; it is to serve the spirit of the tradition and to avoid betraying the object of our inquiry. But what is it to "reduce" or "apperceive" with respect to God? Is it less than to demonstrate, thus involving a lack of certitude? Is it more, thereby yielding to the ontologist illusion? The mind need not abdicate its rights; God need not, to meet the requirements of demonstration, be changed into an object.

Reduction, in the technical sense, is an act, a movement that seeks to pass through the different levels of consciousness [2] in order to secure, step by step, their foundation. It is not a question of a homogeneous regression that would move uniformly from the outside to the inside or from the inferior to the superior. It has to do with a progressive discernment that, acknowledging the specificity of each plane, fashions its own approach; just as criticism, in order to get a grip on each reality, must discern its originality before being able to give a precise determination of its meaning and scope. The difficulty with reduction is that out of respect for the nature of experience, within which it works, it must maintain the solidarity (while distinguishing them) of

1. However, merely by using Husserlian terminology, I do not adopt Husserl's system.

2. The plurality of the levels is well presented by P. Ricoeur in his translation of the *Ideen*, I (Paris, 1950), p. xxx.

subject and object. But if it remains faithful to this complexity, it is not long in discovering that the conversion of the subject implies a corresponding promotion of the object. There is not only parallel progress, but mutual progress. This is why both being and the world have the value of the act that constitutes them.

It is useless, for our purpose, to expose at length the differences Husserl introduces between eidetic reduction, transcendental reduction, and the full act of constitution.[3] We make free use of the vocabulary and example that Husserl provides. The important thing for us is to bring into relief the path taken by the movement of reduction when we go with it to the end of its course.

At the outset, reduction tries to isolate the factual elements so as to consider only essences or significations. For example, it is permissible to take a thousand and one cases of imaginative creation—here the number is irrelevant. It would be a loss of time to focus on the picturesque in each case; the imagining attitude, the essence common to all these facts, is what counts. And we must go further. The signifying attitudes themselves must be appraised separately. When we have suspended in them what is only particular signification, the capacity of posing significations as such will remain. Pure consciousness, the transcendental Ego, constituting intentionality, will be disclosed facing the "world."

If we stop there, we post results that are interesting but insufficient: psychologism is conquered (and all forms of empiricism), the transcendental is established and, moreover, not isolated and separated, but referred

3. We have studied these notions in *Critique et religion*, chap. V. Complementary elucidations will be found in Gaston Berger, *Le Cogito dans la philosophie de Husserl* (Paris, 1941), pp. 44 ff.

to the world, reinstated in the concrete. Furthermore, that which in the natural attitude could only give rise to false meaning and contradiction acquires its true meaning; in particular, the meaning of being is seen, whereas it would have been premature to define it at an earlier stage. Nevertheless, has everyhing been said when the transcendental is attained? No, and Husserl himself concluded by suggesting [4] a hierarchy of three concepts of intentionality: psychological receptivity, noetic-noematic correlation, and finally productive and creative constitution. In other words, after disclosing the transcendental (whose acts are performed by the natural subject, although the latter neither knows this nor even believes in an external cause of its perceptions), we must accede to a deeper plane. How can this be achieved? What will be our course? Undoubtedly, it will be an attempt to reduce receptivity to the limit, in the conviction that it is justifiable only when compared to an originary activity.[5] The discovery of this activity does not entail, however, a reabsorption of the receptive or the received. To make the act soar triumphantly over passivity would be to dissolve the latter and, at the same time, to deprive the act of its point of support. The inquiry then anticipates this act which denies itself an escape and, in the instant of execution, remains solidary with the inferior planes that are necessary to its exercise. In this sense, it can be said that the psychological I is required by the transcendental I,[6] or that the constituting activity in some way gives itself the frames of space

4. Cf. *Ideen,* I, trans. Ricoeur, pp. xxix and xxx.

5. It is known that this tendency belongs to Husserl's early philosophy, the so-called idealist period. But we have taken no position on the whole of Husserl's work.

6. Certain authors, following Kant's *Uebergang,* would say not only *required,* but *engendered.*

and time in which to insert its representations. Secretly, the act prescribes form and content, idea and sensation. It allows itself the luxury of strange misunderstandings when it no longer knows at the psychological plane what it gives rise to at the meta-psychological plane. The act demands what it receives and imposes on itself what is imposed on it. Ultimately, it chooses its complexity and merits its own facticity. We write "ultimately" because, although the transcendental is active in the psychological consciousness, it never emerges there as such. To know its visage, it is still necessary to learn through experience what its fundamental orientation is; only its products express on the outside what it is on the inside.

This last reservation seems to indicate a retreat on our part. For a moment, we were able to appear as timid on this point as Husserl deprived of Fink's audacious stimulations. It is nothing of the kind. To remain at the level of the second intentionality, to refuse to pass to the level of the third (the productive one), would be to hinder the movement of reduction from attaining its end. It has the right to it and demands it; for how can reduction be limited? It set out with a completely Cartesian goal: to find an indubitable which could only be both necessary and absolute. To reduce, then, will consist in tracking down the doubtful, exposing the dependent, the relative, the contingent. To the extent that, within a given, I succeed in discriminating variable elements and, in contrast, a common principle which invariably is found in all the cases, I am authorized to set the first aside so as to better exhibit the second. But this procedure, judged legitimate at the outset, cannot lose its legitimacy along the way. As long as something "reducible" remains, it must be reduced. Practically, as long as receptivity remains, we must progress toward a still more radical act. This is why no one can balk at coming to creative constitution, that is, to the level where, according to Husserl, intuition really gives itself its object. Can we stop there? Does there remain, at the level of this third intentionality, a receptivity or at least a passivity, a dependence or a multiplicity? In our opinion there does. Consequently we postulate a fourth reduction.

In fact, what is this transcendental that is responsible for constitution? Each Cogito is capable of effecting its conversion by taking its own path. But it can then believe either that it transcendentally rejoins an impersonal principle, or that it finds, at its root, a singular intelligible. The first leads to a spiritual monism, the second to an intelligible pluralism, a noetic intersubjectivity. From the perspective of the reductive intention, these two results are far from equal in value.[7] An impersonal principle can individuate; it cannot personalize. That is, it can prescribe, by requiring the assistance of matter, multiple *psychologies* which will be provisional "modes." But it cannot found precisely what is in question: a Cogito that exists only through the reciprocity of other Cogitos, a freedom that awakens and, in any case, opens out only through the mutual recognition of each and every one. But it will be asked if the Cogito and freedom are really that. Is there not a danger here of granting ourselves in advance what we want to prove? It does not seem so. For without even furnishing the complete justification of inter-subjectivity at the intelligible level (we have done this

7. We stress this problem of the status of the intelligible in *Philosophie de la religion,* Part One.

elsewhere [8]), we can and must broach the problem in terms of the relationship of multiple consciousnesses to the transcendental.

Surely no one denies the plurality of psychological consciousnesses. Some, however, hold it to be relative and finally void, the transcendental employing it as a means of expression, at once necessary and precarious. Now, even when the empirical is reduced and the particular significations are suspended, it is a question of knowing whether the Cogito retains its universal fecundity outside reciprocal existence with subjects that function as a worldly interference. We answer no, for the following reasons: a) from the subjective point of view there is position only through opposition, life only through exchange, thought only through common reference and differentiation; b) from the objective point of view there is determination only through negation, and this entails both a multiplicity of notions and a panoramic unity or horizon; and c) from the functional point of view every determination refers to a determinant, and vice versa. Determinations as such imply system, but they can be conceived, compared, and unified around one determination (each in turn becoming the pivot) only if we pose conjointly a plurality of determining principles. The latter must be capable of being universalized through mutual openness, or of becoming, each from its point of view, the privileged center of the entire system. The differentiated multiplicity of the world of ideas has a correlate in the qualified diversity of the community of minds. In other words, there is no determination without a system of determinations (in which each one can be the starting point or head of the whole); but neither is there a

8. Cf. again, *Philosophie de la religion*, Part One.

system of determinations without an intersubjective college (in which each subject is at once a partner and a center). Thus the universal and the singular reciprocally balance and condition one another. Transcendental intentionality no longer says *I*, but *We*, although the plural must be attributed to each singular.

Does a unitary transcendental furnish a more economical solution of the difficulty? Nothing is less certain. If the transcendental were both monistic and impersonal, the plurality engendered below itself would be purely psychological, thus empirical. Intersubjectivity would be only a fall, an accident of fact, a contingent disgrace; it would be illusory and provisional; it would disappear in the light of the purifying reduction. This is why sorting the solutions to this problem imposes an option for one of them. The passage from the one to the multiple that leads from a transcendental monism to psychological plurality cannot be accomplished without loss. The psychological is nothing without the transcendental. If, then, the latter is not itself plural, intrinsically differentiated and singularized, the plurality of the former will only be borrowed, evanescent, and extrinsic. If, on the other hand, the singularity, or rather, the community, of individual minds is founded only on the empirical plane, it will disappear with this plane. From the outset, it will be the illusion of an illusion, having only a phantom existence. To give it power, meaning, and value we must ground it in intelligibility itself.

At this level, the difficulties noted are removed. The multiple is the unity of a plurality of subjects and essences; there is, simultaneously, a college of minds and a system of ideas, a conjunction of universality and singularity. The passage from the intelligible [9] to the

9. In general, I prefer this term to "transcendental."

psychological is conceived in the following manner: subjectivity is really an order, an organic plurality, better, an intersubjective college, wherein persons have their distinct attachment and their own singularity which they express through the diversity of consciousness. A certain fall is inevitable here; it can easily be seen in the everyday experience of the conflict between psychological individualities. At least, personal freedoms retain enough vigor to recover themselves, if they wish, from passivity or hostility. In any case, we see that the confusion of the natural attitude prior to reduction signifies not only a reaction to "mundane" objects (not bad in itself), but complicity with them, complaisance in them.[10] It is neither scandalous nor awkward that each subject has several orders of unequal dignity. The trouble begins when the orders are confused.[11]

However, understanding better the passage from the intelligible to the empirical only displaces our problem; we must still explain what the multiple is generated from. The genesis of consciousness is less disconcerting if it is true that it proceeds from the multiplicity of intelligible singularities to that of empirical individualities, the latter being the expression of the former. Plotinus remarked that plurality, even infinity, is introduced into the intelligible; and it can be held that there are ideas of singular things.[12] It remains, however, to throw light on the appearance of the first multiplicity. If

10. As P. Ricoeur suggests, *Ideen*, I, p. xvii, there is contamination.

11. Perhaps, as Plotinus thought, the sensible is only a cloudy perspective, a fog between the material and the spiritual; its ambiguity makes the psychological consciousness an unstable and confused, equivocal and transitory point of view.

12. Cf. *Enneads*, V, 7, 1, trans. Bréhier (Paris, 1924–1938), p. 123. [English translation by Stephen MacKenna, *The Enneads*, 3rd ed. (London, 1962), pp. 419–20.]

we fail to do this, the question will be insoluble. There will be hope for nothing better than the incoherent thesis of a transcendental monism striving to sustain inconsistent "modes."

Now the difficulty can be handled more easily than one would think. The intelligible, being both one and multiple, exhibits, if not receptivity (a term reserved for the empirical), at least incomplete unity. It is not totally one; it is one and multiple, the active liaison of a diversity, the community of a plurality. And just here the supreme reduction must intervene, leading us in the passage from the *one-multiple* to the *One*.

In fact, how could the intelligible pose itself as an order, at once subjective and objective (spiritual college and system of ideas), if no principle existed from which it could be derived? For whenever, in any given, an even tenuous discrimination can be effected by bracketing the variable elements and discovering the invariant, the reductive movement asserts that derivation is involved. Here, the one and multiple, subjective and objective, characteristic leads inevitably to critical discernment; it is necessary to reduce the staggered arrangement of the multiple and also the subject-object dichotomy. To perform this reduction is precisely to disclose the One as an absolute simplicity, as a truly radical spontaneity that transcends the whole of being and essence. Either one seeks to arrest the reductive effort at a given order (for example that of the *I*, or rather, the transcendental *We*) and is completely arbitrary, since the reducible remains. Or one pushes the purifying exigency the whole way,[13] and establishes that it stops of itself only

13. Maurice Merleau-Ponty writes: "The greatest lesson of the reduction is the impossibility of a complete reduction." (*Phénoménologie de la perception,* 3rd ed., Paris, 1945, p. viii.)

after going beyond all the orders and even the notion of order. God is not an order; he is that by which order can exist.

But does not this trans-ordinal character of God, which is equivalent to calling him the One, render

---

[English translation by Colin Smith, *The Phenomenology of Perception* (New York, 1962), p. xiv.] For the author this formula signifies that if particular objects are reducible, at least the presence of the subject to the world is irreducible. In reality, from our point of view, the world itself is reduced, for *to reduce* is not to suppress but *to grasp as relative*. The world is only the correlate of consciousness. In turn, the subject-object division and intersubjective multiplicity are reducible. In fact, all relation, all diversity, can be grasped as relative to an exigency for unity that is never satisfied. But this exigency, from the moment it is recognized, becomes the sign of a presence. It is not equivalent to the desire for what one does not have; for man, it is equivalent to the capacity for *really unifying*, although his consciousness remains divided and conditioned by the difference of level between subject and object. If man unifies without being Unity, it is because Unity gives him this power, without being confused with him. Thus there is, at the center of the spirit, a simple and infinite energy, an Absolute of liaison and unexceptionable spontaneity. The only *irreducible*, that which has no trace of multiplicity or passivity, is the pure Act. Precisely because an Act and not a supreme determination is involved, God cannot be discovered on the plane of notions, but only at the plane where the subject poses values. To reduce here signifies that one attempts to lead the entire series of determinations back to the unity of a determinant, the free subject. But this latter, paradoxically, is one only by being double, and it is singular only by being plural. In fact, all freedom is exercised through instituting an order, a determinism, a series of determinations (thus there is duality between the free act and its order). And each personal Ego subsists, thinks, and frees itself only in association with all the other personal Egos (thus there is plurality in the Ego, a multiplicity of subjects, and an intersubjectivity tied to the objectivity of a common system of determinations that extends to all subjects). So for a double reason we fail to encounter a simple unity at the level of the transcendental Cogito. For better or for worse, the remaining doubling and redoubling to infinity in human subjectivity must be reduced. If insoluble the difficulty of the passage from pure unity to the multiple unity of the intelligible? Just the contrary is true. Reduction furnishes the proof that essence and existence must be surmounted in order to attain the One. Consequently, the distinction between them applies only to the terms that proceed from the One, and not to the One itself. God is beyond being; he is not less, but more, infinitely more; he is its source. In these conditions, the appearance of the intelligible is also the appearance of being. And, as we saw earlier, this latter

that is done, if we suspend all determination (better, the whole order of determinations); if we in turn place the multiplicity of the determinants between parentheses (this multiplicity attests that each subject participates in subjectivity without exhausting it, and it allows an objectivity to subsist as a divergence between each subject and all the others); in a word, if, within subjectivity and intersubjectivity, we reduce all the determined, the multiple, and the "objective" (and it must be done since each subject transcends determinations from the moment he discovers he is their author, contests the multiple from the moment he sees the non-me as relative to the Me, and surmounts the "objective" from the moment it exists for him), there remains, at the heart of human freedom, only a source of rigorously pure spontaneity. This constitutes a proof that God is really present in man. The proof is there as soon as freedom establishes its effective power to judge all determination derived, all multiplicity reducible, all "objectivity" transcendible. To challenge this proof would be to deny that the free act is trans-determinant. But if it is not, it is no longer a free act. Seemingly, one could be content with saying that the free act separates from the determinations in order to return immediately to them, for it remains situated even when it contests its situation. However, in admitting this "separation," one attests that the free act supports itself on an energy beyond determinations, and that is enough. If man does not escape the determined, although he surmounts it, it is because he employs the Absolute without being the Absolute. *Cogito, ergo sum; liber sum, Deus est,* would be the formula for exhibiting the irreducibility of the One. The proof by freedom, or by the exigency for unity that constitutes the dynamism of the free act, would be the application, pure and simple, of the reductive procedure.

is possible only in correlation with the appearance of essence. At the outset, that is, at the tangential point where the One exercises creative motion, the coming to existence of a community of subjects coincides with the unfolding of a world of essences. Without a subject, no object; without a spiritual college, no system of ideas, and vice versa. In other words, there is no passage to be sought between the One and the intelligible plurality because there is no transition between what is simple and what is composite. God does not communicate something of himself, namely being, to the intelligible (for God is super-being).[14] Rather, thanks to his radical unity, his pure spontaneity, he allows the intelligible to make itself exist, that is, to constitute itself simultaneously as being and essence, subject and object, one and multiple. God presents himself here as the founding productivity that guarantees and conditions the self-position of the intelligible.

The illusion might persist that a similar argument could have been produced in favor of a transcendental impersonal principle of the individual modes. But this attempt is contradictory. It ignores the transcendental's lack of metaphysical simplicity (from which comes the possibility of our fourth reduction). As for the rest, even if the transcendental principle were presumed to be one, it would have only a paltry fecundity; the multiple would appear only at the level of psychological, that is, empirical, consciousness. Consequently, the original unity would either communicate nothing of itself (like the One), in which case the derived multiplicity would collapse into pure psychologism; or it would communicate something of its being (unlike the One), and then

14. Father Sertillanges, commenting on St. Thomas, does not hesitate to call God *Super-Being.*

the equivocation between the two orders would be not only a risk to be run, but an implacable necessity, a necessity of nature. Discernment between the empirical and the transcendental, that is, the very reduction by which the present question could be meaningful, would be rendered impossible.

[II] REDUCTION AND SPIRITUAL CONVERSION

THIS DEMONSTRATION having been made in detail,[15] the way seems open to a new theism. But

15. To relieve the reader's mind, let us summarize. Reduction is employed to discriminate, on each plane of consciousness, the active and the passive, the necessary and the contingent, the one and the multiple. At the first level distinguished by Husserl (psychological intentionality), it sorts the factual given from significations: *eidetic reduction*. At the second level (noetic-noematic intentionality), it brings into view the Cogito and its correlate, the world: *transcendental reduction*. At the third level (productive intentionality), it discloses that intuition creates essences: *constitutive reduction* in the strong sense. At this level, which Husserl hesitated to specify, man is the creator of all determinations. It does not seem, at first glance, that reduction can rise any higher. The third reduction will be the last. However, it cannot be that way, because the transcendental, even constituting and producer of essences, is not perfectly one. It is *one and multiple* (this is proved, as we have shown, by the necessity of maintaining intersubjective and interobjective multiplicity at the transcendental plane itself). After having reduced everything to the transcendental, it remains to reduce that, to disengage the One beyond all determination: a fourth and supreme reduction that can be called *henological*. Thus, thanks to a single reductive intention, close to what Plotinus does in *Enneads*, V, I, 8, we pass successively from the *multiple* (sensations and significations) to the *one and multiple* (the Cogito), and from the one and multiple to the *One* (or God). In all this there is nothing formal or abstract; reduction is not different from the spiritual exigency. When presented with the products of thought, reduction immedi-

undoubtedly, at first view, it will appear abstract or tainted by the dialectical excesses denounced by Kant. It is fitting to respond that reduction, properly understood and directed, is neither a verbal artifice nor a flight beyond spiritual experience. It is a truly concrete act, supporting itself on the initiatives of thought and life that engage the totality of the human subject. Our technical language may appear disconcerting, but we use it only to achieve rigor. Our talk about the empirical consciousness, the intelligible plane, the transcendental, etc., might give the impression that we arbitrarily fragment human spirituality. Critical discernment requires this differentiation of levels of consciousness; but consciousness itself, which is a global and undivided attitude with a unique orientation, produces the diversity of its "orders." There is danger neither of segregation nor of disintegration; on the contrary, these occur only in doctrines tempted to harden the distinction of the faculties into separatism.

The reader may be uneasy on another point. Why have recourse to reduction in natural theology? More specifically, what in the religious evidence invites the philosopher to employ this uncommon procedure? More bluntly: is reduction a genuine demonstration? Must

---

ately interprets thought as productive; and in this latter it detects an impurity, a multiplicity, that makes it necessary to acknowledge, at the core of this production, a more radical act, rigorously one, rigorously pure. If the Cogito were pure act, reduction would not affirm God. Because it is not, because a mixture is still found there, reduction is constrained to go beyond the Cogito itself. Thus understood, reduction reveals in consciousness an energy capable of passing beyond all determination as such. That gives the true measure of the spirit as well as of freedom whose measure, it can be said, is to be without measure, even within a determinate nature and situation.

one hold that religion suggests or imposes it, rather than other "ways" toward God?

These questions, far from hindering our effort, can only confirm it in its results. If we have recourse to reduction, it is because the objective method, when tested, appeared insufficient. We showed earlier that God could not be attained by a simple regression that would put him into an objective series or place him at the summit, making him an order, whereas he is the source of all orders. The God of philosophers that one flatters himself with having obtained by this means is only a first and conditioning axiom, at best a first link in a homogeneous chain of causes. The result is pantheism, or a sort of panlogism that absolutizes the structures of human analysis.

But if only an objectivist approach be admitted as a demonstration of God, it is clear that reduction, which is different, does not "demonstrate." Some would say that it "shows," that it is a eulogy. In our sense, however, "demonstration" involves a number of perils and hardly proves satisfying.[16] Objectivism does not have a monopoly on intellectualism; we feel the need to ground theism in an authentic certitude just as much as objectivism does. Moreover, we believe that reduction, if taken to its limit, possesses by right an irrecusable probative force. It is indeed the only approach, according to us, presenting the degree of rigor suitable to the theistic affirmation. For it alone attains, or rather discloses, a "trans-ordinal" and "trans-categorial" God. The Absolute that it poses, better, that it restores, breaks the circle of anthropomorphism; the relation that joins us to the Absolute is not the Absolute's responsibility but

16. The English here is not so striking as is Duméry's use of "démontre," "montre," and "monstration."—Trans.

ours. Reduction reveals this from the very beginning, thus making unnecessary the intervention of subsequent correctives on such a fundamental point.[17]

Precisely, it will be said; your leap toward transcendence is a gratuitous, arbitrary extrapolation. It loosens up the reasoning on the way; it attempts a jump into the void. If this objection seems plausible, it is only because it caricatures our method. Granted, it is undeniable that reduction, at certain moments, pulls out the blocks, takes off, breaks through threshholds, changes plane brusquely. It never passes from the inferior to the superior by pretending to believe that the second rests on the first as on a foundation which, by bearing it, measures its value, furnishes its raison d'être and its justification. Reduction establishes the contrary; it attains the superior plane only by apperceiving or grasping its emergence, its originality, let us say the word, its transcendence. Consequently, the inferior is found to be suspended from the superior; it resembles, in Plato's words, a plant hung by its roots. There is something here of a reversal of perspective, though there is no question of reversing everything. Simply, the world of perception inverses the intelligible order and the latter inverses pure unity. This necessary restoration, which it effects from itself, is the advantage reduction offers. Far from being a regression that links terms without being aware that they are situated on different planes, it can work as a liaison only if it begins by discerning their different qualities. The connections it effects proceed from its sense for values. And its ascension, far from being homogeneous and linear, is like an alternating

17. It can be said that reduction is intrinsically *apophatic*, in the Dionysian sense; objectivist doctrines of God have this charaeteristic only accidentally.

series of ruptures and bonds. It separates and it adheres; it draws back in order to discern and judges in order to justify its adhesions or refusals.

This is why it must be proclaimed, rather than hidden, that the reductive approach is not at all a mechanical reasoning. It brings into play a type of penetration that Husserl called intuition of essences and that we would call a looking toward rather than a viewing.[18] For, by its exigency for unity, it tends to pass through and surmount the orders, though not to conceal them, still less to soar over them. It requires more than a purely objective rigor that is likely to draw conclusions *vi formae*. It calls for an ever-present attention that is possible only as a function of a spiritual conversion which engages all of man's powers. Purification becomes a condition of lucidity,[19] because the latter demands the renunciation of the direct way and a moment of suspension and retreat which permits the spirit to detach itself from all object and order, even if it must afterwards return to them with new eyes.

If the passage from one order to another already supposes a vigorous initiative, the transcendence of all order, of even the notion of order, demands a redoubled effort. Reduction calls, then, for a purification still more radical, a lucidity still more intense. For there are levels of purification as there are levels of consciousness. Or rather, each level of consciousness calls for an exactly proportionate purification. From order to order conversion takes diverse shapes, each one adapted to the degree of truth and being of the various planes. Particu-

18. Here Duméry exploits the linguistic relationship between "visée" and "vue."—Trans.

19. As Plotinus' formula expresses it: "Without true virtue, God is only a word." (*Enneads*, II, 9, 15, 39–40.) [English translation cited above, p. 148.]

larly when it is a question of breaking with the highest order, so as to suspend it from that by which it is, the risk becomes total. One must be ready to challenge all that one has, all that one is, all being, in order to discover the single incontestable that depends only upon itself and whose only foundation is its spontaneity: the Absolute, the One, God. This attitude is so daring that at this point it threatens all objective security. It severely upsets established habits that hesitate to adopt it or even to consider it correct. Of course it is impossible to make it known to those who do not "realize" it themselves; that would be the same as showing colors to a blind man. The defense of its validity becomes easier when objectivism and its logical techniques admit their insufficiency. In any case, reduction and position of a transordinal God are connected. To repudiate reduction (or any analogous approach) is to forbid theism to attain a living Absolute.

It will be said that this is only a wager, a prejudice. You opt for God, after which you gather in the profits from your option. But such statements expose a misunderstanding of reduction. We do not speak of option, the term being equivocal. Objectivism is accustomed to opposing option, an act of will, to judgment, an intellectual act. Now this opposition implies a separatism of faculties that we challenge. It has the fault of transforming an academic distinction into a metaphysical distinction. For us, both option and judgment refer to the spiritual totality, whose different functions interpenetrate. Thus there is no question of disjoining them, or of using them separately or against one another. This is not to say that we would confound the functions and orders; reduction is always discrimination. Still, this discrimination can only begin through itself. It has many conditions, the complete enumeration of which would be a treatise of full noetic conversion. But it has no distinguishable origin external to it. In fact, on what could we found the conviction that the intelligible order is superior to the sensible? The conviction can be founded on nothing, especially not on the sensible which is just what is denied in order to be transcended. The intelligible must be disclosed by a light that is itself intelligible. And what could found the conviction that the One is beyond the intelligible? Not the intelligible, which is judged to be multiple, relative, and dependent. The affirmation of God, then, must proceed from a particular initiative, more radical than that by which the intelligible fulfills the functions of its order. This is why it must be said that God founds his proof in us. No one can jump higher than his shadow; it is impossible for the intelligible, as a plane of consciousness, to go beyond itself, or even consider itself as nothing in comparison to the One, challenge itself, and know itself to be precarious, if it does not draw this energy [20] from a pure spontaneity that permits it to pull away from the finite in order to judge it to be such. In this sense, there would be only one means of denying God; that would be

20. This energy is present in man since he exercises it. Nevertheless, its origin is higher, since in man it mixes with the obstacles of limitation and multiplicity, with the order of determinations, and with intersubjective confrontation. Since the spirit uses the unifying Unity, everything happens as if the spirit were the One, but the One minus what the spirit itself is, namely, subject-object. This is why we will say the One is both interior and superior to the spirit. In any case, the fact that the One is interior to it, that the unifying Unity is really employed by it, in spite of limits and resistances, proves clearly that acknowledging the presence of the Absolute does not oblige the spirit to go out from itself, to leap into the void, to seek out, by caprice or vertigo, I know not what external and supreme Foundation capable of stabilizing or reifying it.

to affirm that man lacks the capacity either to appreciate his own finitude or to put it in question. But he can do this, and he does do it, each time he recognizes that nothing determinate satisfies him. His demand always goes beyond all that he attains and forces him to proceed further. This is a sign that an infinite dynamism works in him, fading his joys, annihilating his conquests, perpetually placing what he has and is at a distance from what he desires.

Thus we see that the previous objections ignore even the genuine evidence of the problem, somewhat as the natural attitude, according to Husserl, does not suspect the meaning of the questions that issue from the phenomenological reduction. The reduction that leads to theism is especially difficult to describe. At its summit it gathers together the spiritual totality; it recapitulates the successive conversions; it orients freedom toward the only opening where freedom held in a nature could hope to expand itself beyond all nature. Its span is from perception to "ecstasy." [21] This extraordinary breadth makes one think that the very nature of reduction answers to the requirements of religion. This brings us to the other objection that we intentionally brought forward against ourselves: why resort to reduction, rather than to another procedure, when applying philosophical criticism to religious evidence, particularly that of Christianity?

The answer is simple: faith is, by contrast, a short means of going to God, and it has a different completeness than rational demonstration because it aims at the possession of God. It skips over reasonings, dispenses with having to make them; moreover, the ordinary man could not make them. If learned men argue, even

21. In the sense of union with God.

though they believe, it is perhaps for a pedagogical or apologetical end. If it is because of a philosophical need, they find themselves side by side with the other philosophers and must submit to the same rules. If it is proved to them that objectivism does not hold, they must seek something else, that is, a procedure without the same difficulties—in these circumstances, reduction. Besides, the name matters little; only the reality it designates is important. Recourse to the reductive approach is justified above all by the necessity of resolving a problem that does not yield to other methods. And it has this double benefit: it requires the philosopher to revise his logical tools; it places the believers in front of their responsibilities when they wish to philosophize. It frees each one to return to the problems he prefers, on the condition that he is at least aware of the presuppositions these imply and the results they inevitably lead to.

The use of reduction is, however, justified for another more pressing reason that by itself would be determinative. If religion affirms two things strongly, they are the existence of God and his transcendence, two things that also interest the philosopher. Consequently, philosophy must be able to criticize them in the same sense that the religious man takes them; otherwise, it will use the same words to treat a completely different problem. It is a fact; each time philosophy attains a notional God rather than a trans-ordinal God, it betrays and disfigures the evidence that it ought to understand before criticizing. Moreover, it achieves only ridiculous results with respect to the exigencies of the practical (which makes one doubt that it has realized the scope of the problem in the lives of men). That is already a sign that the philosophical work has been badly conducted. Above all, it is a proof that the

distinction between religion and philosophy has been
badly formulated. In fact, the theist who ends up with a
God not clearly separated from the objective series that
supports his demonstration begins by confusing philosophy with a logic that is prisoner to empiricism and also
with a type of wisdom that is, instead, some form of
positive science. Or he holds that philosophy should,
with the aid of discursive operations, project certitude
onto the objective plane where all rational construction
occurs. Now that is a triple prejudice of empiricism,
positivism, and objectivism, all of which can be reduced.
Taken together they are only variations of the natural
attitude. On its side, independent of any particular
position, philosophy must be brought back to its true
role. It is a critical method applied to the creations of
spontaneous thought (crude or sophisticated); it is not
living spirituality. The spirit (as act) and concrete
reflection (not secondary reflection) act and structure
experience. Yet, since there are overly zealous people
who sometimes end up by mixing apparent values with
genuine values, and confusion with rigor, the products
of living spirituality must be submitted to critical
examination, to philosophy. The latter, in order to
describe what it discovers, will appear to construct; in
reality its primary task is to prune and separate the
valid from the false or incomplete. In this sense, the
philosopher, like the scientist, engages in but a single
type of construction; he elaborates complicated and
subtle instruments in order to bring to light the implications of the real and to verify whether in fact spiritual
experience respects its own norms.

This is why, concerning the Absolute, philosophy
has no other task than to criticize *the way thought* (or
living spirituality) *proceeds when it wants to prove the*

existence of God to itself.[22] It involves proof and criticism of a proof; but not substituting itself for the agent responsible for the demonstration, namely, the spirit itself. Now in fact and by right (faith set apart), the spirit succeeds in proving God only by surmounting the sensible and the intelligible, by understanding that they are not self-sufficient. But that is nothing other than the reduction lived and thought before philosophy learned to name and formulate it. Undoubtedly, philosophy does more than photograph this event of thought. Philosophy makes it appear to reflective consciousness and by that gives it a new breadth. But without the effective act that guides and sustains this effort, secondary reflection would find itself without an object. In order to clarify the proofs of the existence of God, the spirit first of all must place itself in them, impregnate them with its exigency, and breathe its vigor into them. The spirit is supported less by them than they are supported by it. Or rather, as we have said, it supports them on this influx that carries it beyond all that it is.

If one agrees to this, which seems to us undeniable, then philosophical theism and religious theism are no longer antithetical. They are not identical, for faith is specific; [23] but neither are they in competition. Religion

22. It perhaps would be more precise to say: *his presence.*

23. Without infringing on what would have to be said to characterize faith itself, we must note that the religious initiative has its own manner of effecting the reduction. The notion of charity, in a Christian context, designates a pure love of God that delivers the soul from all partiality and prevents it from attaching itself to any determination as such. We have developed this point in *Foi et interrogation*, pp. 36 ff. Consequently, the movement of the soul amounts to passing through each particular order, to making it free from any finite object, and also even from itself. Thus it is equivalent to a real challenge of all having and being; it is the fully liberating reduction in act. In short, charity does *practically* what reduction verifies *critically.* Thus we are

fears no encroachment, and philosophy is no longer
reduced to being content with the "God of philosophers."
The latter was only a conceptual artifice to satisfy easily
pleased minds or to prevent all rational intrusion into
the domain of the sacred. There is no longer any place
for these expedients. The spirit goes where it can; of
itself, it tends toward the Absolute. Mystery is not
violated because the spirit can only intend the One by
way of the multiple, that is, by way of what it does and
is. It falls to the philosopher, in any case, to examine the
initiatives of the spirit and to sift them; he will remind
the spirit what is of worth and what is not. But by
allowing the spirit to show its full capacity, he will see
the theistic affirmation constituted little by little. The
spirit will produce it; the philosopher will judge it.

[III]   REDUCTION AND WAYS TOWARD GOD
         (ONTOLOGICAL PROOF AND PROOFS
          THROUGH THE SENSIBLE)

IT WILL BE UNDERSTOOD, consequently, why
we have urged the reduction. It reveals itself to be the
best means of respecting living spirituality. Without
threatening the original character of faith,[24] it makes

---

justified in thinking that reduction, in spite of its technical
appearance, does nothing other than bring to light the source of
religious conversion and the dynamism that carries the spirit to
the threshold of mystical experience. That suggests how much
our method can owe to a reflection on the spiritual life.

24. For faith, the category of the Absolute is reinforced by
that of mystery, at the same time that the scheme of transcendence is closely allied to the schemes of revelation. Criticism
would tend to be principally interested in what, in the affirmation

the theisms of the philosopher and the believer rein-
force, instead of obstruct, one another; for both proceed
from the living spirit. The advantage of this is that God,
for both philosophy and religion, is no longer in the
"category of the ideal." He can only be the living God,
and not merely the idea of God,[25] about whose reality we
can never be sure.

---

of the religious categories, permits going beyond them in the
direction of the Infinite (God discovered in the specificity of
truth). The religious man, on the contrary, prefers to move into
the chiaroscuro of historical signs, uncovering one part of the
divine mystery. But this opposition must not be pushed too far. It
is the duty of the philosopher of religion to comprehend the
alternation of unveiling and veiling that makes the religious
subject take revelation now for an attestation, now for a
protection of mystery (secularized in Heidegger this alternation
can become a theory of truth, the counterpart of an ontology).
Perhaps the philosopher can understand this dialectic better than
the religious man since the latter lives it without reflecting on it.
Thus the philosopher keeps himself from confusing mystery with
a fund of truths having God as proprietor, or with a secret for
which God would be jealous. For God is not an ensemble of
determinations beyond our grasp. The mystery comes from us
who make the screen, not from God who is pure light. When we
believe we unveil him, we veil him, since we compromise his
unity. In this sense, God is the simple that we complicate, the
One that we render "complex," the Absolute that we "relativize."
This is why revelation leads to him only by detours; it rejoins him
only after inquiring across situations or clarifications that are
ours and that in no way constitute a divine past time during
which a greedy Infinite would take pleasure in projecting himself into the finite. With these remarks we intend to make clear
why we limited ourselves to examining the notions "absolute"
and "transcendence." The categories of mystery or revelation can
be studied only in relation to the religious evidence. Or rather,
they can be clarified only through the clarification of this evidence. Concrete revelation is entirely expression and schematism,
whereas mystery both yields itself and escapes, declares itself and
remains unspeakable.

25. This comes down to recognizing, as we have said, that
God cannot be held in any determination.

The ontological proof has already attempted to handle this difficulty. It was unsuccessful; or it succeeded only by relying on the prior conviction that God cannot be an idea among others, a concept taken from the ensemble of determinations. One can think him only by receiving power from the Infinite himself,[26] so that the passage is no longer from the idea to the being of God, but from his necessarily lived presence to his existence freely and consciously acknowledged.[27] Still, in order to be entirely correct, proponents of the ontological argument would have to furnish explicit proof of the failure to hold God in a concept, to enclose him in the objective series of determinations. Without this initial demonstration they would not be able to convince their adversaries that every idea of God is the expression of his real existence. They would seem to give themselves gratuitously at the beginning what they want to find at the end. Unless, like Descartes, if Gueroult's interpretation be admitted,[28] one takes care to rest the

26. Malebranche writes, "The Infinite can be seen only in himself, for nothing finite can represent the Infinite. If one thinks of God, he must be." (*Entretiens sur la métaphysique*, 2nd Entretien, ed. Paul Fontana, I, Paris, 1922, p. 47.) [English translation by Morris Ginsberg, *Dialogues on Metaphysics and on Religion* (New York, 1923), p. 90.] See equivalent formulations in *De la recherche de la vérité*, ed. Lewis, I (Paris, 1946), pp. 248–55. [English translation by T. Taylor, *Father Malebranche's Treatise concerning the Search after Truth* (London, 1700), pp. 119–22.]

27. In reference to the ontological argument used by St. Bonaventure, Gilson writes, "Saint Bonaventure does not pass from the idea to being, since for him the idea is only the being's mode of presence in his thought. Thus there is no real transition to be effected between the idea of a God whose existence is necessary and this same God necessarily existing." (*La philosophie de saint Bonaventure,* 2nd ed., Paris, 1943, p. 110.)

28. Cf. *Descartes selon l'ordre des raisons,* I (Paris, 1953), pp. 345–46. "It can be concluded that the location of the ontological

ontological proof on the proof through effects. But this amounts to making the decisive apperception depend on an *a posteriori* reasoning,[29] as if reduction, to adopt our terminology, could rest on its inferior supports.[30] In reality, exposing the One in his purity coincides with our awareness of the multiple as multiple (or of the finite as finite and the imperfect as imperfect). But it is the capacity to challenge all finitude and all determination that implies a pure spontaneity; the latter *explains* the former, not the inverse. If someone would say that to judge finitude as such proves only that one carries in himself the idea of the Infinite, or even that one is himself infinite, we would have to respond that reduction does not allow this way out. For precisely the reductive intention demands the passage to the One only because the spirit aspires to a unity, or to a perfection, which the *one-multiple* of the Me lacks. This proves that if I have the idea of the Infinite, it is of an Infinite that I seek to rejoin, not of an Infinite that I am able to be.[31] To aim at

---

proof suffices to show that it is not the first truth, but a second truth; that it depends on the proof by effects as on a higher reason; that it is without value when isolated; that it presupposes reasons not needed by the proof through effects; that the proof through effects is the fundamental proof of the existence of God and, in fact, the only one . . ."

29. This reasoning requires, as Gueroult clearly shows, the simultaneous use of the principle of causality and the principle of correspondence (conformity of the idea of God to its ideal). Cf. *op. cit.*, pp. 171 ff.

30. In fact, Gueroult would not deny in the least that for Descartes God's emergence into the spirit does not occur in the understanding which is finite, but in the will (author of judgment) which is infinite. There one can persist in placing a self-affirming presence of the Absolute.

31. Gueroult, commenting on Descartes, gives a similar answer to this difficulty. "The certitude of always being able to go beyond the degree, whatever it may be, of perfection that I have attained, attests that I am bound to finitude. And, to suppose that

the One is always to go beyond self and every thing while remaining multiple and finite, that is, to remain where one is although tending toward the beyond. At any rate, whatever be the upward course, it draws its power from the Absolute, not from the steps it climbs. And that exempts us from prefacing the supreme moment of the reduction with an auxiliary and preparatory argument founded on a chain of concepts. Nevertheless, the Cartesian defense of the idea of God as a unique case, in which essence and existence are necessarily fused, remains valuable. Is it not one way of establishing that the idea of God differs from every particular determination? [32] This is how Descartes' example remains suggestive, even to one who is inspired by other principles.

---

thus I potentially have the Infinite leaves me no less incapable of producing the objective being of the idea of the Infinite that is an actual being, since a potential being is nothing. On the contrary, the aspiration toward the Infinite that is absent from us supposes the objective reality of the actual Infinite and supposes that the idea of the Infinite issues from our faculty of amplifying all created perfections in order to construct the idea of God; yet this faculty of conceiving the greatest thing is present only because we have in us the idea of a greatest thing, namely, God himself." (*Op. cit.*, pp. 189–90.)

32. Although the necessities of language force us also to speak of the *idea* of God, we never start off from an idea, whether it be of the Infinite, the Absolute, the Perfect, or the One. We make a critique not of an idea, but of a concrete initiative accomplished by the living subject. This initiative maintains itself on the plane of real operation even when the reductive procedure reflects it on the ideal plane. This is why it does not give rise to an existent after starting from a determination (something that is strictly impossible). It is content with discerning a pure Act at the interior of a mixed act, an integral spontaneity within a spontaneity tainted by the multiple, one that is seen to be inwardly divided from itself since consciousness is obliged to mediate its existence through an essence and its action through a reflexive doubling.

On the other hand, Kant's objection (following that of St. Thomas, but in another context), that the idea of a necessary Being remains a possibility, misunderstands one important thing. It arbitrarily reduces the idea of God to a particular determination. In fact, if the idea of God has a meaning, it is that of unity or simple perfection or pure spontaneity.[33] Now, any determination is essentially plural; it is contrasted negatively to a whole system. Far from being a determination, the idea of God is rather, as unity, that by which all determination is conceivable at the level of organizing thought, that is, thought that must surmount the multiple. Or it is that without which no determination would be conceivable. Moreover, it is easy to see that the rejection of the ontological proof does not rest only on a refutation *ad rem*. Rather, it is the consequence of initial positions, foreign to the guiding preoccupations of the partisans of that celebrated argument. One author juxtaposes concepts obtained by abstraction from the sensible and at the same time divides all substances into essence and a proportionate act of existing, a principle which is then generalized and extended to the totality of being. Another decrees that an idea is valid only through liaison with a given sensation and that, consequently, every concept of a supra-sensible object remains unverifiable in the eyes of pure reason. It can scarcely be seen, in the

33. Later, after the critique of the divine attributes, we will understand better that our idea of God is necessarily below God. It has a functional role; for taken as a determination, it is only the conceptual expression of the intention toward God. Thus it remains human, limited, ambiguous, indefinitely purifiable, even when the movement of the soul it takes account of is supported by an Absolute of exigency. This Absolute impels man to place himself totally (essence and existence) in question in order to transcend himself in all that he has and is.

first case, how the idea of God could be kept in the conceptual register at the moment generalization extrapolates or poses a pure Existing for which the distinction between essence and existence is no longer meaningful. It is even more difficult to see, in the second case, what justifies the initial decree, if it is not the prejudice of adopting scientific reason as the pattern for philosophical reason.[34]

Nevertheless, for the first case, our severity must be softened and even changed into a happy surprise. Recourse to the Aristotelian problematic would have led Christian thought to an impasse. The genius of St. Thomas, his power of integration, his respect for the tradition (particularly Pseudo-Dionysius and Augustine), led him to temper the logical instrument received from Aristotle. How, in fact, does he proceed? His five ways are built upon abstraction from the sensible. He starts from facts in order to reach an Existing who founds existents. But he does more and better than this; if he had limited himself to a *de facto* question, he would not have been authorized to conclude *de jure*. In his demonstration, over and above observation or induction, he employs genuine metaphysical principles, in

34. It will be noticed that our method does not consist of reviving the ontological proof, although it has an air of kinship with it. We are seeking neither to connect synthetically essence and existence in God, nor to pass from his idea to his being. We are seeking to disclose the exigency for unity, present in every determination, that leads all the way to the One. To refute us, one would have to establish that man's exigency for unity is neither sincere nor real, but only pretense. However, starting the reduction forces the denial of this hypothesis; to think, to act is always to unify. It is only a matter of knowing how far, by right, the unifying impulse goes. Our thesis consists in showing that it can find its point of equilibrium only in arriving at the One.

particular that of causality under various forms.[35] If, for
example, he begins by declaring that everything moved
is moved by an other, then asserts that only an unmoved
mover can be the reason for moved movers, he finishes
by concluding that this self-mover, or first mover, is
what we call God.[36] This logical series has several
significant steps. Let us specify them.

First of all, the passage from what is moved by an
other to the self-mover, from the *ab alio* to the *a se*, can
be effected only by one who realizes that the *ab alio*
implies activity and passivity, the former irreducible
(because positive), the latter reducible (because negative). Next, the affirmation of the self-mover coincides
with the discovery of aseity, or pure activity, that cannot
be surmounted; any further pursuit would be vain since
the end found offers no handle for a subsequent reduction. Finally, the identification of the first mover and
God [37] attests that the signification bestowed on the *a se*
includes something other than a content relative to the
action exercised on and in us by God. For example, we
are certain that God exists because, as Creator, it is

35. In E. Gilson, *Le Thomisme*, pp. 85–119, will be found the
exposition of and references for the five ways. [English translation cited above, pp. 59–83.] We suppose they are known to the
reader.

36. Here Kant saw the unacknowledged intervention of the
ontological proof. Cf. *Critique de la Raison pure*, Transcendental
Dialectic, chap. III, section 5, trans. Barni-Archambault, II, p. 140.
[English translation cited above, p. 510.]

37. Raymond Ruyer cites S. Butler's observation that "the war
the deists and atheists made with each other was caused by the
question whether it is necessary to call God "God," or to give him
another name." (*Néo-Finalisme*, Paris, 1952, p. 1.) This bit of
humor makes it quite clear that in order to name God "God" one
must have specific reasons—among others, that the Absolute
must not be designated by any name that can be suitable for
relative beings.

possible to perceive his effects in us. But this is not to say that he is only the author of these effects. He is, on the contrary, infinitely more, this being signified by the passage to pure activity, that is, to an inexhaustible spontaneity, which it is impossible to enclose in the limits of a given achievement, even the whole of creation. Thus the Thomistic demonstration implies something other than mechanical conjunctions; it is made up of living initiatives, of successive reductions that are, so to speak, latent and faint. If St. Thomas did not draw them into prominence for our use, it was not by mistake. It was undoubtedly because in his time comprehension of metaphysical principles had a quality of immediacy akin to the conclusions of common sense. On the other hand, by constantly beginning from the sensible he hides the fact that he reasons on experience instead of submitting to its pressure.[38] If he lets himself

38. Over and over again, Brunschvicg ("Religion et philosophie," *Revue de Métaphysique et de Morale*, January, 1935, p. 8; *Le progrès de la conscience*, I, Paris, 1923, pp. 113–16; *La raison et la religion*, Paris, 1939, pp. 55–58; *Héritage de mots, héritage d'idées*, Paris, 1945, pp. 56–57) reproaches St. Thomas for concluding beyond his premises. We would say, to the contrary, that St. Thomas is conscious of posing in his premises much more than appears at first sight (namely, all that will burst forth as conclusion). For example, where a surreptitious and illegitimate passage from the finite to the infinite, or the imperfect to the perfect, is denounced, it must be said that, in order to be able to pose the finite or the imperfect as such, it is necessary (by means of an implicit reduction) to lean on the notion (or rather, the reality) of the infinite, the perfect, which is primary because positive and justified only because self-justifiable. On the other hand, if St. Thomas rejects the ontological argument, possibly it is because in order to lead to pure Existing the reduction must deal with an existent and not an abstract notion (nevertheless, the thesis of St. Anselm or St. Bonaventure would be that God is not an abstract notion). Thus we do not believe that St. Thomas committed a paralogism by concluding too much; nor did he beg the question by giving himself too much at the outset. For to

be taught by sensible experience, it is because the objects it presents are not opaque things, but beings provided with an essence and an existential act that already witness to the pure Existing. So St. Thomas is not aware of submitting to a meaningless reality, nor does he wish to submit to psychological subjects, that is, those ignorant of their metaphysical dignity. As a good theologian, he intends to obey only God, who measures both the intelligible and intelligence.[39]

reduce is always to discover what is already there. At the most, it could be lamented that the logic of Aristotle, which St. Thomas had the audacity to adopt in spite of fierce opposition, constrained him to fit approaches that imply genuine spiritual initiatives to the mold of an objectivist terminology. More particularly, when he affirms that every effect supposes a cause, he limits himself to the immediate evidence of this principle; here he appears to lay himself open to Brunschvicg's objection which reminds us that every effect has a cause, but a cause of the same order. Likewise, if St. Thomas says that the ascent through causes must be stopped, Brunschvicg retorts that nothing obliges us to do that, since we are moving in a homogeneous context (the series of causes being of the same order): "that there is causality *in the world* does not prove a causality *of the world.*" In fact, St. Thomas leaves unmentioned an operation that he really performs: he attains a cause superior to the created effect because he proves himself capable of reducing the passivity contained in the effect and finding support for it in an irreducible—pure activity. He ascends to God, not simply as author of the effect, but as pure Act that extends beyond all conceivable effects. The urgency to limit the ascent is present because the irreducible does not let itself be exceeded, rather than because of the necessity of choosing an ultimate cause in order to set a limit to the enumeration (that would be an empirical and gratuitous decision). Brunschvicg's position is very carefully defined by Marcel Deschoux in *La philosophie de Léon Brunschvicg* (Paris, 1949), p. 181. That St. Thomas does more than he says or says less than he does can be either praised or regretted.

39. One of the difficulties with St. Thomas, writes Fernand Van Steenberghen, stems from "what L. Becker . . . called the 'dialectical shape' of his thought, or more explicitly, the continual interferences of the logical order in the real order, the tendency

If St. Thomas gives his proofs, or to use his exact term, his ways toward God, a spiritual climate,[40] the other Christian doctors have the same concern. We do not need to retrace the history of their thought. Let us point out only that St. Bonaventure, heir of Augustinianism, achieved an approach quite similar to reduction [41] one that, moreover, is very close to the ontological

to express ontological relations through the detour of relations that are true only in the order of logic. . . . For the most part, St. Thomas is not duped by this manner of speaking that he borrows from his milieu. But this fault, so characteristic of a culture saturated with dialectic, caused many headaches for his disciples. It is surprising that this aspect of scholastic thought has scarcely been studied up until now." ("A travers la littérature thomiste récente," *Revue philosophique de Louvain*, LII, 3rd series, no. 33, February, 1954, pp. 128–29.)

40. We have taken up again, from the point of view of reduction, the first way. It would be possible to do the same with the other four: efficiency, contingency, degrees of being, and finality, although in each case reduction risks appearing more or less compelling. We believe that the fifth way would be the least suited, and the fourth the best suited, to reduction. Curiously, in *Ideas*, I, Husserl provides a reason for using the order of the world, thus of favoring the fifth way (cf. trans. Ricoeur, p. 191, n. 2). Husserl's context is clearly different from that of Thomism. [The note referred to is a commentary by Ricoeur on Husserl's §58, "The Transcendence of God Suspended"; Ricoeur refers as well to Husserl's Note to §51, English translation by W. R. Boyce Gibson, *Ideas: General Introduction to Pure Phenomenology* (New York, 1931), pp. 157–58.]

41. "Quomodo autem sciret intellectus hoc esse ens defectivum et incompletum, si nullam haberet cognitionem entis absque omni defectu?" *Itinerarium mentis in Deum*, III, 3; minor ed. (Quaracchi, 1925), p. 317. [Duméry subsequently published his French translation of this work, *Itinéraire de l'esprit vers Dieu* (Paris, 1960). The above text appears on page 65 and can be rendered into English as follows: "How, in fact, could our intelligence know that a being is deficient and incomplete if it had no knowledge of the being without lack?" English translation by George Boas, *The Mind's Road to God* (New York, 1953), p. 24.] Cf. the citation and commentary, as well as complementary texts, in E. Gilson, *La philosophie de saint Bonaventure*, 2nd ed., p. 108.

argument already mentioned. He asserts that it would be impossible for us to think the imperfect or the negative if we had no knowledge of the perfect or the positive of which they are the privation.[42] The proof of God is thus governed by the reduction of the imperfect and by the apperception that the idea of the perfect conditions the efficacious awareness of all deficiency.[43]

Since our own recourse to reduction has profited from notions not so very different, it shows itself to be traditional.[44] Since reduction is practiced more or less

42. The same reasoning is in Bossuet, Élévations I and II, éd. Garnier, pp. 5–8.

43. St. Bonaventure holds, moreover, that the divine being, when thought of in itself, has an absolute evidence: "it is because the necessity of the divine being is communicated to thought that a simple definition can become a proof." (E. Gilson, op. cit., p. 109.)

44. In fact, three principal conceptions of God have appeared within historical Christianity: 1) the Dionysian tradition, characterized by a dynamic apophaticism; 2) the Aristotelian tradition, which came late but became the most official for instruction; 3) the Augustinian and Malebranchian tradition (of Platonic origin, but with the Ideas placed in the Word). Moreover, these three tendencies interpenetrated and gave rise to many combinations. But the first is the oldest. In Christian Antiquity, it was not solely of Pseudo-Dionysius' making. St. John Chrysostom insisted strongly on the incomprehensibility of God (Cf. his sermons on this subject in the collection, Sources chrétiennes, Paris, 1951; in the introduction prepared by Fathers Cavallera and Daniélou will be found, in addition, references to Basil and Gregory of Nyssa as well as Justin, Clement of Alexandria, Irenaeus, and Origen). After Pseudo-Dionysius, we must cite Scotus Erigena, Eckhart, Nicholas of Cusa (cf. De la docte ignorance, trans. Mouliner, Paris, 1930, pp. 98–100) [English translation by Fr. Germain Heron, Of Learned Ignorance (New Haven, 1954), pp. 59–61.] and in general, the minds inclined to mysticism. If we have defended a kind of apophatic reduction as a way toward God, it was not to deny the pluralism of Christian natural theologies. Rather, we have done it on the conviction that any religious theism, whatever problematic it prefers, is obliged to have recourse, if only surreptitiously, to other methods than objectiv-

consciously by Christian thinkers, recovers the attitudes
of the religious soul, and is sheltered by living spirituality, the philosopher of religion cannot avoid encountering it. By putting it to use, he enriches philosophy
without burdening faith. Whereas other methods need
additional notions such as analogy to preserve the
Absolute from the repercussions of an ontology that
risks reinserting divine causality into derived causality,
we will show that, for reasons intrinsic to the reductive
method, reduction respects the divine mystery much
better.

---

ism. We have drawn a certain inspiration from Plotinus' doctrine,
but that is not to say that it served as a point of departure. In
fact, it was through criticizing the anthropomorphism of certain
theistic systems that we were thrown back toward the apophaticism of the One. For us, Plotinus was an indirect encounter.
Besides, many Christian authors, even without having read him,
were able to be spontaneously in agreement with him. Cf. E.
Gilson, *La liberté chez Descartes et la théologie* (Paris, 1913),
pp. 185–86.

III / Ontology or Henology?

Now IT IS TIME to undertake our study of the scheme of transcendence. Until it is criticized, all reflection on the nature of God remains at the mercy of the imagination. In an important passage of *Ideas* I, Husserl states that the transcendence of God must be left unconsidered because, unlike the pure Me, it is not given "in an immediate unity with the reduced consciousness." [1] He wants to say, from his point of view, that the transcendence of God, even immanent to consciousness, is not one with consciousness the same way the Ego is one with its activity of thought. Consequently, God's transcendence must be set aside, although, when the essentials of pure consciousness are described, it is impossible to suspend the question of the Me. Even if we do not adopt Husserl's prudence on this point, we do receive valuable guidance from it. God's transcendence is different from both the transcendence of the world to consciousness and that of the pure Me to thought. That is why we introduced earlier the epithet *trans-ordinal*, which suppresses all equivocation and

1. Cf. *Ideen*, I, trans. Ricoeur, pp. 191–92. [English translation cited above, pp. 173–74.]

underlines the pure unity of God in contrast to the multiple unity of the "orders" of consciousness. Simplicity is the privilege of God because he is radical spontaneity; in order to be one, he does not need to project from the other or stretch toward the other. He escapes any dehiscence which would introduce otherness, that is, a constitution of orders or planes. He remains superior to all disjunctions like essence and existence, act and potency, form and matter, etc.

[1] PURIFICATION OF THE SCHEME OF TRANSCENDENCE

BUT HOW CAN the human subject, incapable of surmounting itself and leaving the region of consciousness, think transcendence? The subject necessarily employs imaginative schemes to support the category of the Absolute and, if not to conceive it, at least to represent it.[2] The term "transcendence," psychologically elaborated with reference to spatial data,[3] can

2. These schemes are multiple, and they are variable. Each one in its manner is a scheme of transcendence. It would thus be proper to speak of several schemes of transcendence. If, nevertheless, we use the singular and not the plural, it is because all the particular schemes of transcendence serve as auxiliaries to the same spiritual intentionality. We are interested in what is common to all these schemes, not in what particularizes them imaginatively. Anyone who wishes to consider their diversity (as well as their complementarity), can refer to Maurice Nédoncelle's paper, "Sur l'évolution de quelques métaphores relatives à la transcendance." (Cf. *Actes du XIe congrès international de philosophie*, XI, *Philosophie de la religion*, Brussels, August 20–26, 1953 (Louvain, 1953), pp. 97–103).

3. Cf. Th. Ruyssen, "Transcendance et immanence; Essai d'interprétation psychologique," *Revue philosophique*, nos. 10–12, October–December, 1951, pp. 492–529.

be purified of its relation to exteriority only with difficulty. In addition, once the trans-ordinal character of
God is admitted, we must no longer speak of transcendence. Jean Wahl, following Hartmann,[4] suggests that it
would be more suitable to say *trans-ascendence*, or
movement from what is transcended toward what transcends, or again, *trans-descendence*, or superiority of
what originates yet remains independent. At any rate,
the image is still borrowed from space and, as such, can
be reduced.[5]

Do we then conclude that the notion which it
accompanies must also be reduced? Must we speak of
the Absolute without specifying that he is transcendent?
In order to escape extrinsicism must we run the risk of
sinking into immanentism? It is not a simple question
of language. According to whether one admits or refuses
to name transcendence, religion—and philosophy too—
change scope and even nature. For without transcendence there is no longer a genuine Absolute, that is,
perfect unity, truly radical spontaneity. Religion becomes incapable of raising man above himself or the

4. Cf. *Bulletin de la Société francaise de Philosophie*,
October–December 1937; cited in J. Grenier, *Le Choix* (Paris,
1951), p. 59. [Perhaps the reader of this translation will find
Wahl's book more readily available: *Existence humaine et
transcendance* (Neuchâtel, 1944). A modified version of Wahl's
lecture is found in pp. 34–51, and the Appendix, pp. 113–59,
presents extracts from the extensive and valuable discussion
which followed.]

5. The realistic (external) beyond and the soul-substrate
obviously are schemes taken from primitive thought. Cf. Marcel
Deschoux, *op. cit.*, pp. 193 and 200. That would suffice to
discredit them in the eyes of Brunschvicg. The latter, however—
and we will come back to this—never ceased to be obsessed with
this problem. In *Progrès de la conscience*, for example, he insists
on it nearly with asperity. Cf. 1st ed., pp. 760, 763, 778, 779, 782,
783–86; cf. especially p. 783, where he speaks of God and the
mind as two subjects of inherence placed face to face.

world and of inspiring him to efficacious charity. Philosophy, in its turn, in spite of the élan of living spirituality, becomes incapable of commanding the supreme reduction which attests that the intelligible order itself is derived. Be that as it may, the movement of the spirit cannot be limited. Religion will always claim the right of being acosmic to some extent. And criticism will let itself be intimidated by no prejudice. For better or for worse, it is necessary to "reduce" until one discovers a total simplicity in which there is no longer anything to objectify or go beyond, because it is in fact, to use Jacques Paliard's word, the *indépassable*.[6]

But we do not have to go over that again. A trans-ordinal Absolute has been proved; the reality of transcendence has already been brought to light. It cannot be rejected, for the reason that it alone guarantees the authenticity of the Absolute disclosed by reduction, any absolute-object inserted in a series of orders being contradictory. It is only a question of knowing if and how transcendence can give up its spatial scheme and retain a spiritual signification.[7] We

6. Cf. "Prière et dialectique," *Dieu vivant,* no. 6, p. 55.

7. Let us note in passing that transcendence seems to be opposed to *immanence,* as the outside to the inside. In fact, the transcendence-immanence correlation was able to appear only quite late in philosophical language. The term *immanent* (an Aristotelian idea and in opposition to *transitive*) has a much earlier (although uncertain) origin than transcendent (cf. the history of these terms in Lalande's *Vocabulaire,* 5th ed., Paris, 1947, pp. 453 and 1120–21). At any rate, the authors who admit transcendence never make it exclude the immanence of God to the spirit. Quite to the contrary, they hold that the transcendent God is *also* immanent. Only the thinkers who translate *transcendent* by "exterior" and who, in addition, confine immanence to the psycho-rational operations of consciousness, are accustomed to rendering divine transcendence and immanence antinomical, even incompatible.

will show that it can and must do it; for, contrary to what Brunschvicg believed,[8] the sole means of radically challenging objectivism is to recognize, on one hand, the specificity of a non-hypostasized intelligible order, and on the other hand, the transcendence of an Absolute that is in series with no "order."

Brunschvicg instituted the famous opposition of "on one side, the realism of transcendence born of an *arrogant* imagination; on the other, the idealism of immanence that proceeds from a reflection in depth." [9]

8. Concerning Brunschvicg, one remark must be made at this point. He rejects as a dangerous myth any idea of transcendence. But does he realize that only since relatively recent times has this idea, when applied to God, been supported by the contemporary spatial scheme? For example, the Medievals never feel the need, once having demonstrated God, of specifying that he is transcendent; it follows from itself, since to them a God reduced to the level of reason would have seemed contradictory. Certainly well before the Middle Ages neo-Platonism had the notion of, or at least the word, transcendence; it was borne by a spatial scheme analogous to ours. The One, for example in Plotinus, is said to be ἐπέκεινα νοῦ, beyond intelligence (*Enneads* V, 4, 2), as God, in Pseudo-Dionysius, is declared ἐπέκεινα πάντων, ὑπέρ πάντα κατὰ τό ὑπερούσιον ἀπολελυμένος, ἐπέκεινα, τῶν ὅλων (cf. Migne, *Patrologiae Graecae*, 872 A, C and 1048 B; trans. de Gandillac, *Oeuvres complètes du Pseudo-Denys l'Aréopagite*, Paris, 1943, pp. 145, 146, 184). [English translation by C. E. Rolt, *On the Divine Names* and *The Mystical Theology* (New York, 1920), pp. 151–54 and 200–01.] It is clear that the prepositions ἐπί and ὑπέρ (Plato, *Republic* 509b, already placed the Good ἐπέκεινα τῆς οὐσίας) are originally references to space. But it is also clear (in Plotinus, the movement of the fifth *Ennead* proves it forcefully) that going beyond intelligence and essence is only a passage to pure simplicity, a reduction of the multiplicity at the interior of the *one-multiple* that the intelligible is. There is not exteriority but interiorization. The loss of interiority does not come from conversion to the One; it occurs because multiplicity appears within the intelligible itself, and even more within empirical consciousness.

9. *De la vraie et de la fausse conversion* (Paris, 1951), p. 127. On the following page, Brunschvicg reproaches St. Augustine for

This antithesis, which cuts between two imaginative types, is, however, artificial. If to draw from what is higher is to depart from the mind, it goes without saying that we would repudiate this materializing extrinsicism. Moreover, what does it mean to work in depth? The spirit, which has no outside, is also without thickness. And the method that seeks an objective sub-conscious as it would seek an external super-conscious fails to meet the demands of a philosophy of interiority whose function for us, as for Brunschvicg, is "not properly speaking to explain, but on the contrary, to comprehend."-[10] But let us leave these schemes in their picturesqueness. The beyond and depth are metaphors of the same quality; if not transcended and corrected, their literalness would harden into error. There is no reason for adopting one image rather than the other. On the contrary, there is a pressing need to judge the ideas they recover, or rather discover, for us.

Now it turns out that the first (the beyond), purged of its physical realism, tends to signal the primacy of the Absolute, which cannot be in series with other beings.[11]

----

juxtaposing "brusquely, not to say brutally, the *illuminism* of the interior God and the *extrinsicism* of the transcendent God." St. Augustine's procedure is treated elsewhere as "impenitent eclecticism." (*La raison et la religion*, p. 48.) But Brunschvicg always stresses the spatial character of the scheme of transcendence, to the point of speaking of "cosmic transcendence" (*De la vraie . . .* , p. 132). See the comments of Marcel Deschoux, *op. cit.*, pp. 192 ff.

10. In its context, the formula is applied to mathematics (*De la vraie . . .* , p. 165). It can also define a fundamental aspect of Brunschvicg's method inasmuch as it poses as a method of comprehension and self transformation.

11. This expression is Spinoza's (letter to Jarig Jelles), and is used by Brunschvicg from his point of view (*De la vraie . . .* , p. 166). We will see that it would be better placed in a perspective of genuine transcendence. [An English translation of Spinoza's

And the second (depth), so effective for eliminating exteriority from the principle of unity, is incapable of suggesting that this principle has originality in relation to the transcendental plane. Brunschvicg, however, is aware of this and places pure unity and the universality of reason, as organizer of the real, at the same level. By doing this he fails to make the supreme reduction, which is imposed for the reasons we gave earlier. At the same time, he contradicts himself, at least implicitly. For if the One is identified with the transcendental, there is—contrary to what would be thought—a greater risk of putting him in series with consciousness. In fact, it is not sufficient to establish that God cannot be called *other*, in the sociological sense, or be made one term beside another, as in arithmetical addition. It is certain that God cannot be added to us, either as a quantity to a quantity, or as a quality to a quality. Nevertheless, this does not say enough; alongside these correct observations we must place another. Precisely because God is nothing that can be numericaly added to anything else, we must refrain from making him a principle which, even though placed in the spirit, would respond inadequately to the demands of personhood. If he is confounded with the transcendental, he becomes an impersonal principle that remains juxtaposed to persons. In this respect, if he is not, strictly speaking, in series with them, he remains foreign to them; [12] he is incapable of

letter appears in *Benedict de Spinoza; His Life, Correspondence, and Ethics*, ed. R. Willis (London, 1870), pp. 360–62.]

12. As pure form he cannot be in series with subjects. And because he is incapable of founding their singularity, he remains, in spite of everything, extrinsic to it. A directly personalizing intelligible does not present this difficulty. But it must be situated below the One, therefore specified as a unique "order," distinct from the One and the empirical Me.

founding and justifying personality. For this position persons are no more than evanescent modes, simple products of the illusions of the biological Me. In addition, there is no means of interpreting the fact that this unitary transcendental engenders the subject-object division as well as intersubjective plurality. Unity, suddenly lowered to the plane of the one-multiple, becomes an impoverished, broken, unstable unity that cannot lay claim to the simplicity beyond all determination. Thus the identification of the One and the transcendental breaks up into confusion and incoherence.

The argument, however, seems to come back against us. If God is distinct from the intelligible (or the transcendental), how can we avoid saying that he is in series with it? Does one not add items that are identical? Not here, because the terms are not of the same order. Addition is impossible and illegitimate [13] because *God and the intelligible do not constitute two orders, but the absence of "order" and the presence of an "order."* [14] God can be only if he is trans-ordinal. To *add* would be to include God in a series in which terms of the same nature are added; this would destroy even the notion of the Absolute. And it is to be noted that we can no more add God to things than things to God. In neither one sense nor the other can one add that which makes planes to THAT BY WHICH consciousness, in order to constitute itself, distributes itself into planes. The best

13. Cf. the quite definite formulas of Plotinus, "the One refuses to be numbered in with any other thing, whether it be with one other unity, or with an indefinite number." (*Enneads* V, 5, 4, trans. Bréhier, p. 95.) [English translation cited above, p. 406.]

14. On the contrary, the transcendental, or as we prefer to say, the intelligible, is an *order* because it is one *and* multiple, subjective and objective plurality.

way to avoid putting God in series with us is to keep from reducing him to our level, even the highest one; this means to think him with reference to no level, that is, to pose him as *trans-categorial*.

But here it will immediately be asked how we can break out of our categories, or if that can even have a meaning. In fact, who has ever succeeded in doing it? St. John of the Cross, wrote Henri Delacroix referring to J. Baruzi's study, "went beyond only an inferior form of the intellectual life. The mediation that his contemplation surpasses is not intelligence. How could he claim to have really surmounted intelligence?"[15] If such an approach were possible, would it not be a grave offense to the mind? Here again Brunschvicg finds the formula: "the categorical imperative of consciousness is to not let itself be transcended; mind is interiority, or it is not."[16] No one can simultaneously serve spirituality and transcendence; to be transcended is to be denied. To place pure spontaneity in God is to deprive ourselves of our own light, to evict ourselves from our own home, in short, to commit suicide as a spiritual subject. The accusation, it can be seen, is particularly serious.[17]

15. Cited maliciously by Brunschvicg, *De la vraie . . .* , p. 191.

16. *Ibid.*, p. 188.

17. Perhaps Brunschvicg formulates it only because his idealism lacked the notion of intentionality. By using this notion we understand that God can be *intended* by consciousness without the latter having to abandon itself in order to attain him. According to the schema of "the process of revelation" that we give at the end of *Critique et religion,* God is intended only through categories, schemes, and from the general "situation" of consciousness. Transcendence toward God is a recovery, a gathering together, an orientation of self that makes maximum use of man's resources at the instant he recognizes that the object of his intention can be confounded neither with what man is nor with what he himself does on his plane.

Fortunately, it misunderstands the true implications of theistic transcendence. Let us unfold these implications; exposing them will be our best response. What in fact follows from affirming a trans-ordinal God? Paradoxical but enlightening consequences. A new ontology takes form, one which preserves both the divine primacy and the originality of derived beings. No rivalry between the Infinite and the finite is to be feared. God does not steal our subjectivity; he does not stifle the substance of man.

[II] BEING AND THE ONE

IF GOD is the One, pure simplicity, absolute spontaneity; if he is neither an order nor a plane, but that by which planes and orders are possible; if he escapes, by dominating it, the distinction between essence and existence, as well as the subject-object disjunction; if, in a word, he is not Being but, according to a neologism taken from Dionysian language, Super-Being,[18] it must no longer be said that the terms proceeding from him receive a part of him. They do not borrow from him the being that they are, because he is not. Strictly speaking, he communicates nothing to them. Thus, with respect to being, we can follow certain

18. I have already noted that Father Sertillanges used the expression *Super-Being*. Maritain reproaches him for thus exaggerating our incapacity to know God. Cf. *Les degrés du savoir*, 3rd ed. (Paris, 1932), pp. 827 ff. [English translation supervised by Gerald B. Phelan, *The Degrees of Knowledge* (New York, 1959), pp. 425 ff.]

mystics and call him Nothingness or Nothing.[19] There exists no direct participation [20] between the One and beings; without correctives or expedients, that would lead to pantheism. The relation of God to the created cannot be defined by an ontological transmission, be it total or partial. Being, in fact, need not submit to transfer and does not reside in God; it appears only at the level of the created and is found contemporary with the multiple, the finite, and the imperfect. Let us say then (a) that the One furnishes, to the term that proceeds from him, the capacity of being what it has to be, and (b) that the One is not. This reveals the One's mode of productivity and also the necessity for the immediately inferior term (the intelligible) to confer being on itself. The One cannot give derived spirituality, of any sort whatever, something of what he is, because he has nothing and is not.[21] The One can only give it the

19. Plotinus called God the *One* only because he lacked the term zero (cf. E. Bréhier, *La Philosophie de Plotin*, Paris, 1928, p. 161, note 1). [English translation by Joseph Thomas, *The Philosophy of Plotinus* (Chicago, 1958), p. 157.] Scotus Erigena called God *Non-Being* (cf. *De divisione naturae*, I, 3, in Migne, *Patrologiae Latina*, 122, col. 443 A–C; commentary in *Jean Scot Erigène* by Dom Maïeul Cappuyns, Paris, 1933, p. 338). [English translation by Charleen Schwartz, *On the Division of Nature* (Quebec, 1961).]

20. Maurice Nédoncelle presents numerous equivocal senses of this term in *La Réciprocité des consciences* (Paris, 1942), pp. 29–34.

21. Simone Pétrement observes that the "God who is not" risks, in a sense, favoring atheism, because "separated, unknown, detached from all," he "appears to be without power and nearly nonexistent." But she adds, "in another sense, dualism is perhaps the only theism, because the 'God who is not' is perhaps the only God." (*Le dualisme dans l'histoire de la philosophie et des religions*, Paris, 1946, p. 120, note 1.) We do not see this dualism between the *God who is not* and *that which is,* for the reason that

radical aptitude to give being to itself; in other words, to pose itself, to make itself. In this sense, the One creates by rendering self-position possible and participation impossible.[22]

To take the other side, if God were called *Being*, and not the *One*, procession would once again be ontological derivation, thus participation. Each derived term would imply the same act of existing, which would restrict it in proportion to its own essence, this varying with the substances and serving to define them and establish a hierarchy among them. God could recover his transcendence only by the timely adjustments provided by analogy. He would become pure Existing and as such would be immanent to all existence. Yet, at the same time, he would be transcendent to it, since the essence added to the latter introduces the finitude by which

---

the first is not in series with the second. But it does seem correct to us to affirm that the super-being God, that of Plotinus and Pseudo-Dionysius, that equally of the fifteenth-century author of the *Nuage de l'inconnaissance* (cf. Armel Guerne's translation, "Documents spirituels," no. 6, *Cahiers du Sud*, Paris, 1953) [*The Cloud of Unknowing*, ed. with an introduction by Evelyn Underhill, 3rd ed. (London, 1934).], that even of Lagneau (for whom being and existence are not proper to God, cf. "Cours sur Dieu," in *Célèbres lecons et fragments*, ed. Michel Alexandre, Paris, 1950, p. 250), is, so to say, more absolute (the only absolute) than the Being-God, who can be placed above determinations only by means of supplementary correctives. The famous verse, Exodus 3, 14 (I am He who is), is not given as a metaphysical definition; above all, it expresses the refusal to name God. It can serve a negative theology as well as an ontological theology. In addition, let us recall that saying God *is not* does not insinuate that he is less than being; rather, it proclaims that he is more.

22. Everything considered, supernatural grace is "participation" (in the technical sense defined above) no more than natural illumination (with different degrees of gratuitousness) is. It is preferable to conceive it as a passage from *self-position* to *Aseity*.

resemblance and difference are mixed together in being. There is participation in the existent, but restriction as well; for participation is gradual and graduated, with beings set at intervals along a series in which a common element, being, is distributed at infinitely diverse levels. In any case, the opposition is clear between this *participationist* ontology and *processionist* ontology. In order to sum up the antithesis, it could simply be said that *ontology* has *henology* as its contrary,[23] defining them as follows: the first holds that the inferior borrows a part of what it is from the superior; the second holds that the inferior receives from the superior the means to be what the superior is not.[24] In the one, there is communication; in the other, there is literally position of self-position.

23. I write *henology* with an *h* out of respect for the Greek etymology (Gilson, however, writes *énology* as one speaks in politics of *Énosis*). I believe that I have discovered a precedent in the historians of neo-Platonism who write *hénade*. In his *Vocabulaire* (5th ed., p. 397) André Lalande gives *hénothéisme*.

24. Gilson has brought out this antithesis remarkably well in *Le Thomisme*, 4th ed., pp. 193–200 [English translation cited above, pp. 136–41], and *l'Être et l'essence* (Paris, 1948), pp. 38–45. This can be judged from the following passages: "The chief characteristic of the philosophy of Plotinus is that it is built upon a metaphysics of the *One* rather than of Being. To affirm that the One is the first principle of everything that is, is to admit at the outset that the One is not a being. . . . A superessential God is not, therefore, a being. Indeed he is much more than a being, and precisely because he is more than a being, he is not a being. This amounts to saying that God is a non-being, and that the *non* ὄν or 'what is not' is the supreme cause of all that is . . . the One, which precedes being, contains within itself all the being which itself is not." (*Le Thomisme*, pp. 194–95.) [English translation cited above, pp. 136–37.] And there is more. "To speak of being *à propos* of God, is not to speak of Him but of His effect . . . being is but the revealing or manifestation of the One; in a word, its 'theophany.' As to the One, it remains *ante* ὤν: it is not entangled in the order of its participations." (*Ibid.*, p. 196.) [English translation cited above,

p. 138.] "In a system in which being proceeds, not from Being, but from the One and the Good, one enters simultaneously into the order of being and into that of participation." (*Ibid.*, p. 198.) [English translation cited above, p. 139.] Also, there is the following: "The One is not being, and precisely because it is not it, it can cause it. . . . The so-called pantheism of Plotinus is a perspectival illusion which stems from mixing two heterogeneous ontologies . . . it is not a question here of comparing two ontologies, but an 'ontology' with, one could say, an 'énology'. . . . In a doctrine of Being, the inferior is only by virtue of the being of the superior. On the contrary, in a doctrine of the One it is a general principle that the inferior is only by virtue of what the superior is not. In fact, the superior always gives only what it has not, since, in order to give that, it must be above it." (*L'Être et l'essence*, pp. 40, 41, 42.) In the same passages Gilson gives the principal references to Plotinus and Pseudo-Dionysius. The rest can be found in Jean Trouillard, *La purification plotinienne* (Paris, 1955), and René Roques, *L'Univers dionysien* (Paris, 1954), or by reading directly *Enneads* V and VI and the *Divine Names*. The fifth *Ennead* is the strongest text in the whole history of philosophy in defense of the specificity of the intelligible. A careful reading permits the conclusion that Plotinus does not have the "floating conceptions" of the soul and the subject that certain authors attribute to him. Gilson, who put us in his debt by setting up the antithesis between *ontology* and *henology,* draws some surprising personal conclusions, notably that henology leaves existential ground in order to lead the subject to a plane of salvation through knowledge alone. This point of view is at least open to discussion, because knowledge in neo-Platonism does not have the partial and abstract character of a reflection cut off from life. In a Christian context, ontology has certainly been influenced by the *Ego sum qui sum* of Scripture. But this expression, which we spoke of earlier and whose meaning is periodically put in question (cf. A. M. Dubarle, "La signification du nom de Iahweh," *Revue des sciences philosophiques et théologiques*, XXXV, no. 1, January, 1951, pp. 3–21), can have only derivative philosophical importance. Henology retains the privilege of rigorously preserving the transcendence of God, the essential affirmation of the Judeo-Christian tradition.

[III] CONSEQUENCES OF THE CHOICE
FOR HENOLOGY

THE CHOICE BETWEEN ontology and hen-
ology must be made in full consciousness and clarity,
for the consequences are heavy and the responsibility is
immense. Without playing down any of the quite real
advantages [25] of ontology, it must be agreed that henology succeeds in safeguarding *together* the radical
productivity of the One and the creativity of the intelligible.[26] This is no insignificant gain. The benefit is
threefold: 1) The Absolute enters into competition with
no order; in no respect is he an order; he is only pure
energy, "fontal" [27] principle. 2) The spirit is found to be
responsible for the deployment of the orders. 3) We
render void the complaint that would make the affirmation of the One an impossible movement outside consciousness. In fact, the activity that permits the spirit to
pose itself by posing its own objects resides in it, and in
it alone (the One has neither determinations nor an

25. For example, the advantage of affirming the originality of
the act of existence in relation to essence. Here Gilson's
interpretation of Thomism will be recognized.

26. Gilson finds a similar conception in Gibieuf, an Oratorian
theologian of the seventeenth century. "For Gibieuf, as for
Descartes, God is first of all an infinite power of production from
which proceeds all good and all existence. Like Descartes, he
refuses to recognize even a shadow of distinction in God or to
break up his perfect unity by introducing inclinations, reasonings,
deliberations, and choices. Finally, also like Descartes, he places,
at the origin of the world, a creative power whose activity is
deployed entirely in the order of efficient cause and not at all
in that of finality." (*La liberté chez Descartes et la théologie,* p.
199.)

27. An epithet found frequently in St. Bonaventure.

objectifying consciousness). Nevertheless, the Absolute can be the source of all because he is not what beings are.[28] As the hyper-ontological principle, he dominates the ontological determinations situated at the level of the derived spirit without being in series with them. Being is only the trace of the One; but it is the trace because between it and the One is interposed (if we may say so) the active mediation of the intelligible. The One gives his motion to the latter; however, this motion breaks into the open only when taken up by the intelligible. The trace of the passage, or rather the presence, of the One is thus marked, thanks to a specific initiative of the spirit. When one holds simultaneously that *the intelligible has to make itself intelligible* and that it affirms God, not as something of its order but as that which permits the intelligible to pose itself as order, where is the sin against interiority? It is the *I*, and not God, who is law to himself in the sphere of his operations; autonomy corresponds to self-position. But it remains to show (the final reduction does this) that self-position is possible only through an absolutely pure and irreducible spontaneity, namely, the One. The latter is discovered at the root of the spirit, at the point where the superabundant indetermination of creative motion takes form and singularity by returning itself, if we may say so, toward its principle. Thus the intelligible is constituted in this self-determination which is freedom —freedom obliged to pose an order of determinations,

28. God is foreign to all genus, specifies St. Thomas (cf. *Sum. Theol.*, I. a.q.4:a.3.ad 2, ed. *Revue des Jeunes*, I, *Dieu*, p. 136) [English translation in A. Pegis, ed., *The Basic Writings of St. Thomas Aquinas* (New York, 1945), I, p. 41.]; he does not go so far as to declare that God is not inserted in the series of transcendentals: being, truth, goodness.

but authentic freedom intrinsically oriented toward the One, that is, wholly inclined toward absolutely pure Freedom.

All things considered, it seems to us that transcendence is a positive notion, which can be thought in spiritual terms. It would be easy to mock because of the spatiality of its scheme.[29] But can a single notion be cited without involving time and space? The purest categories need to be supported by schemes that effect the liaison between the understanding and experience. No doubt the possibility remains of a relapse that progressively materializes the idea. The contrary is equally true: at its level, critical purification can either recover the idea or replace it. We have tried to do that by presenting the transcendent as trans-ordinal. That led us to the discovery of a new ontology, or rather a hyper-ontology, that refutes in advance the objections against transcendence. Brunschvicg saw threats to interiority everywhere. He held that the affirmation of a Transcendent led immediately to the notion of being, which introduced realism. He reproached Plato for not having succeeded "in defending the purity of ascending analysis, of *participation in the One*, against the opposing tradition of descending synthesis, of *participation in Being*." [30] But it turns out that these two kinds of participation, which Brunschvicg in one sense rightly opposed, do not dance just the figure that he supposed.

29. Brunschvicg concludes by combining anathema and jest. The transcendent and extrinsic God becomes the God of spelling opposed to the God of arithmetic, that is, of intrinsic truth or spiritual immanence. Cf. Marcel Deschoux, "Les vues pédagogiques de Brunschvicg," *Les Études philosophiques*, new series, sixth year, no. I, January–March 1951, pp. 92–98.

30. *Le Progrès de la conscience*, II, p. 792.

Some further clarifications on this question, in order to confirm our opinion that it is necessary to admit a transcendent God, will not be superfluous.

Between the ascending dialectic toward the One and a descending dialectic starting from Being,[31] there is room for a third approach, *procession,* which substitutes henology for ontology. The opposition is not between regression and progression, both of which refer to the One. It is between two forms of ontology, one founded on the notion of Being, the other on that which goes beyond it and justifies it. Brunschvicg is wrong not when he subordinates Being to the One, but when he believes that all processive dialectic is confounded with an ontological generation that implies the anthropomorphism of finality and the objectivism of hierarchical criteria. We are spared this confusion. There are no determinations *pre-posed* in the trans-ordinal God; he has no need to conceive in order to perform. Thus the philosopher need not seek the "divine plan," still less the psychology, the secret intentions, or the ulterior motives of the Creator. Only the intelligible brings about the appearance, at its level, of multiple determinations which, linked together, constitute an order. From God to the intelligible there is no transmission of essences, but only derivation of energy; this shows that procession is neither an empirical synthesis nor an analytical deduction. Rather, there is in it a sort of *a priori synthesis* which, in the name of an ideal necessity, connects terms that are enriched by mutual rapprochement. But strictly speaking, it cannot even be said that procession is

31. In *Philosophie de l'action,* I spoke of descending dialectic in a different sense; that was because Blondel gives God the name of Being. Nevertheless, Blondel specifies that to ontology he prefers an *ontogeny* whose norm has axiological value.

synthesis, particularly if we adopt Brunschvicg's understanding of synthesis as an imaginative flight out of experience. There is not, and need not be, synthesis in the proper sense, even *a priori* synthesis, when one tries to pass from the One to the intelligible. There is no passage, because there is no common intelligibility between the two. The intelligible is an order constituted through contact with the One, but at an inferior level. Even later, in the descent from the intelligible to the sensible, there is no *a priori* synthesis,[32] since this passage records no growth of the intelligible. We have established elsewhere,[33] that the sensible is an expression of the intelligible, even an inversion, that is, a reversed or confused expression. In any case, we are far from a direct ontological communication. If the One is called *cause* and the intelligible *effect,* it must be maintained that being does not pass from the cause to the effect. It appears only with the effect. On the other hand, if the intelligible is called *cause* and the sensible *effect,* it is proper to affirm that being is in the cause and that the effect is responsible for expressing it. Still, we must note that being is in the intelligible because it is measured by intelligibility, and this latter is the correlate of an intellectual *act.* We thus have the surprise of encountering being only at the intelligible level; it proceeds from the One, that is, remains inferior to it, and makes the sensible proceed, that is, remains superior to it. Thus understood, being is changed into a

32. There can be, on the contrary, *a priori* synthesis within an intelligible order where the whole and the parts are linked according to an ideal rigor that allows the universal and the singular to coexist. In consciousness this *a priori* synthesis shows through each time an operation, theoretical or practical, rejoins the intelligible.

33. Cf. *Philosophie de la religion,* Part One.

norm. It serves to structure sensible experience and to valorize spiritual experience in its ascent toward the One. This is a sign that the primary aim of progressive dialectic is to found regressive dialectic, or a sign that progression supports conversion. In Brunschvicg's terms, we would say that descending creation (which would be relieved of its bias for physical explanation) is meaningful only when regarded as the condition of ascending creation which is growth in the orders of truth and love.

We must not, however, believe that conversion erases procession, that the return annuls the going. In that case, the neo-Platonic schema would be only a puerile image. In reality, procession is less an unfolding of orders, done once for all, than a persistent will to specify the uniqueness of these orders. For example, at each instant the intelligible must continue to be what the One is not. This is why even when the intelligible finds itself in the process of conversion, even when it prepares itself to perform the supreme reduction, *it must still proceed*. It realizes itself by turning toward the One, but because it goes out from the One. To be able to bring itself back to the One, it must first of all proceed from the One. Thus conversion never abolishes procession; it leans on it and witnesses to it.[34] When conversion attains, procession maintains; when conversion leaps over, procession establishes; when conversion unifies, procession specifies.[35] They are two solidary and

34. When conversion rejoins the One, acknowledging the source from which it proceeds, we can say that it completes, consecrates, and thus maintains, procession.

35. Jean Trouillard gives the true formula: "consciousness realizes itself by *detouring* from its origin, thought by *returning* toward it." (*La purification plotinienne*, p. 96.) [The French edition incorrectly refers to p. 126.] The first is procession, the

complementary movements which are geared to one another and are mutually stimulating. They can be neither suppressed nor disjoined without the whole collapsing into confusion or inertia. But in addition, they are possible only as functions of a trans-ordinal God who founds, not an ontology, but a henology. Only a transcendent Absolute can dominate the orders. Only he can permit them to constitute themselves through themselves, with the degree of efficiency that corresponds to their degree of truth. Without transcendence there is neither pure spontaneity nor simple unity, that is, no Absolute. But also there is no creativity, there is no efficacious freedom in man, no real inventiveness in the world. The refusal of transcendence thus becomes a return to positivism. Positivism is glorious in other respects, but unless it is unfaithful to itself, it must be content with objectivism.

---

second conversion. But there is no consciousness without thought and no thought without consciousness, at least for the terms that "proceed." Thus we can understand the solidarity, through the alternate (more profoundly: *simultaneous*) mutual promotion, of procession and conversion. If the cogency of these remarks is acknowledged, Brunschvicg's objection to grasping God falls of its own accord. At the instant the spirit touches the One at the summit of conversion, it is no less distinct from the One, since procession constantly brings it back within its order. To rejoin the One is to aspire toward presence to him without ceasing to rest under him, that is, at the intelligible level, the first degree of procession.

IV / Negative Theology

ALL PERIL is not averted. New dangers appear for our unexpectedly firmed-up position. Once a trans-ordinal and trans-categorial God is exposed, an unanticipated reef rises. If God is made a superessential simplicity, if he excludes the system of determinations, if he ceases to be the place of ideas (which enter at the intelligible plane), in short, if he is truly transcendent, are we not thrown back to agnosticism? Brunschvicg would observe, with good reason, "The unknown God is unknown as God, just as the human God was mistaken for God." [1] Or again, mocking Plotinus, who said of the One, "We say what it is not, and what it is, we do not say" (*Enneads*, V, 3, 14), "Negative theology, if it has a meaning, can only signify the negation of theology." [2] In these conditions, what would be the purpose of talking about that which we do not know? The zeal applied to defending transcendence would only have demonstrated the uselessness of the notion "absolute." We have no

1. *Héritage de mots, héritage d'idées,* p. 63.
2. *La raison et la religion,* p. 110.

need of the refractory; for that which is refractory and impenetrable is also unthinkable. Practically, agnosticism reduces us to atheism.

Religion offers here an apparently simple solution. God is known to us in the dialogue he maintains with us; he reveals himself in history by transmitting a message which teaches us something about himself and very much about ourselves—in any case, enough for us to be able to work out our salvation and to turn his grace to account. But that is precisely the issue; can a transcendent God be an Absolute of dialogue? It seems that by definition the answer must be negative. This places us in the uncomfortable situation of one who, in order to obey one command, violates another. Desiring to save the transcendence that religion affirms, we have compromised the dialogue between God and man that religion also affirms. Is there possibly a third way between agnosticism and anthropomorphism? If so, what is it? We need to know it to get out of our impasse.

[I] THE PROBLEM OF THE DIVINE ATTRIBUTES

WITH WHAT are we concerned here? Is it with qualifying God, describing him, if we may say so, from his point of view? That makes no sense at all. The citation from Plotinus that we just recalled by way of Brunschvicg, and which, through Pseudo-Dionysius, was inscribed even in the *Summa* of St. Thomas, gives these pretentions their due. As the Medievals were fond of saying, God is *uncircumscribable;* one can neither contain him, nor surpass him, nor in any manner (and this is the decisive point) *objectify* him. Our effort to disentangle the notion of God from the regressive homogeneous web has led us to acknowledge that he transcends the distinction between essence and existence and by this transcends Being itself. To serenely define his attributes is a deception. Here an affirmative "theology" meets its limits.

But in fact it is not a question of determining the indeterminable, of describing the ineffable. The question is whether God is cut off from us, or if a tie does unite us to him and how it can do so. Now we have previously disclosed this bond of the mind to God by showing that the intelligible order constitutes itself through contact with the One. Consequently, the problem comes down to exactly this: how to recover, at the plane of criticism, the meaning and value of the relation of the mind to God. Critical reflection will justify the duty of progressing, so to speak, to the interior of this relation, in the direction of God. Or rather, because the presence of God is already implied in the progress itself, the duty of advancing will be revealed as a double and simultaneous fidelity: to self and to God. It can already be guessed how divine transcendence and spiritual immanence can be linked.

No, we do not know what God is. But we do know that it is necessary to affirm him because his presence is undeniable. We also know that the intelligible proceeds from him and aspires to rejoin him. In other words, we know that the mind has an intrinsic relation to God, a *living relation*.[3] In us, spirituality is the encounter of

3. Father Ortégat asks, "Can something beyond human thought be known without an intrinsic orientation toward that Beyond?" (*Philosophie de la religion*, II, Louvain, 1948, p. 675.) His answer, and ours, is no. Only the relation to God within the spirit permits the latter to have some knowledge of the Absolute.

divine motion with a resistance capable of differentiation; it is the superabundance of the One overflowing at
the level of finitude, where he restricts himself and
breaks into light. By the same token, the illumination
interior to the spirit is the revelatory sign, par excellence,
of the presence of God. And religion is nothing other
than conversion to this illumination, which conditions
the ecstasy to come [4] and serves it as both a base of
departure and a base of control.[5] When the spirit is
understood as relation to God, religion and spirituality
are identified, provided that the life of the spirit can
receive from God not only a capacity for self-
determination, but the still better aptitude of liberating
itself from all determination. The specific purpose of the
problematics of the supernatural is to safeguard the
possibility of this aptitude.

If this is so, it is the same thing for the spirit to
constitute itself (by posing ideas and values) and to live
and exercise this relation to God. God gives the spirit the
possibility of *acting* so it can give itself *being*. To accept
the first, to confer the second on itself, to go toward God,
are three different ways of designating the same fundamental operation. Thus it can be understood that being
turned toward the Absolute (being converted) coincides

4. We do not, as does Brunschvicg, make religion the cult of
rational light, because there is something superior to this light.
But if we speak of religious experience, taken as a whole and
carried to its limit, we can say that accepting grace implies
discovering the intelligible light (which exposes the inconsistency
of the inferior orders) and also recognizing our ignorance of the
divine (center of energy or pure freedom).

5. For judgment must remain, so that the entry into mystic
darkness is entry into an excess of light rather than a return to
the obscurities of the sensible. As Brunschvicg puts it, we must be
able to decide "whether clarity does not become darkness,
whether the night is not illuminating." (*De la vraie et de la fausse
conversion*, p. 267.)

with correctly performing the tasks of the spiritual function. Conversion regains the benefit of procession. This suggests to us what religion is in its essence: the active discovery of God as source and end—as ever actual source and perpetually moving end. We can specify further. The spirit does not submit to this source; it lives from it by acting through it. And this end does not remain exterior to it; the spirit prescribes it to itself, since it is through contact with the One that the spirit becomes spirit.[6] Thus by posing its laws, by imposing its norms on itself, the spirit grasps and wills itself as oriented dynamism; it is *for itself* only by also being *for God*. We have a paradox only because we are dealing with a theocentrism of the One; that is, the spirit is attracted by an absolutely simple principle that can be compared neither to a force nor to any power of impulsion (force and power being comprehensible only within complex systems). But this is a new proof that the polarization of the spirit by God is completely immanent, to the point of being identical with spirituality itself.[7]

6. Gabriel Marcel remarks that "the spirit poses God as the poser." (*Journal métaphysique*, p. 46.) [English translation cited above, p. 46.] From our point of view, we would say that the spirit poses God as that which gives it the means to pose itself.

7. This position can be better understood if we note its neo-Platonic (Plotinian or Erigenian) antecedents. For Plotinus and John Scotus Erigena, it seems that God can perfectly be the One without creating (thus he is transcendent); but because he is a *Nihil per excellentiam,* he cannot know himself (knowledge implying detour) without creating. By creating spirits that aim toward him, he creates being and thought in them. They, being given this intention, leave their mystical indetermination and create themselves as spirits by making themselves theophanic in the most rigorous sense. The intelligibles ("formative reasons" in Erigena) are really created in the common act through which God and the creatures express themselves. Thus summarized (in

With that as a starting point, it will be less daring to presume that the true knowledge of God consists not in grasping the divine object,[8] but in correctly implementing the procedures at the disposal of consciousness for both realizing itself and relating itself to its principle, accomplishing itself and offering itself. More briefly, to know God is to know oneself as spirit, dependent spirit. Or again, in technical terms, it is to perform the reduction, to pass from the *one and multiple* to the *One*. There is the impossibility of knowing the unknowable, but also the need to recognize, to live consciously, the relation of the spirit to the One. Now this can be done, at the level of criticism, only by instituting the series of real approaches by which the spirit detects, interprets,

---

modern terms, because Plotinus refused to speak a creationist language, whose artificial schemes he rejected), neo-Platonism appears to anticipate Hegel. However, in contrast to Hegelianism, transcendence is never compromised, in principle or fact, by the neo-Platonists. The One necessarily transcends his expressions, even if the latter answer to a law of procession that he freely imposes on himself. For ourselves, we avoid adhering too closely to the neo-Platonic terminology for fear of encouraging a misunderstanding. Since emanationism is too often confounded with necessitarianism (which leads to immanentism), we have been careful to adopt a different vocabulary. We are anxious to affirm with absolute clarity the gratuitous character of creation and to give the greatest possible prominence to the notion of transcendence. We can be grateful, nevertheless, to the neo-Platonists for disclosing the self-creating role of the spirit and for marking so forcefully the intimacy of the relation that binds each spirit to the One.

8. How can the simple be known, when the knower himself is complex; the One, when he remains multiple; the Infinite or the Perfect, when he remains finite and imperfect? It seems that the only way is to *intend* the Absolute by way of the relative, God by way of the human. This is precisely what is done by religion and, in general, the spontaneous subject. When one knows how to intend God, one knows how to rejoin him, and that says sufficiently what he must be for consciousness.

and assumes this relationship. We will not have an explanatory "theology," but rather the effort by which the spirit tends toward God, and the critique of this effort. We will lose nothing in the exchange: the first, too ambitious, would be deceiving; the second, by its modesty, will keep us within our limits while providing the guarantee that our intention is steadily focused on the unknowable God. We are not in God, but God is in us and we belong to God. It is by deciphering the meaning of the acts that concretely lead us to discover him that we will perceive how not to falsify him.

We do not need to make up a list of these acts. They all belong to the supreme reduction and maintain its efficacy.

Let us take an example. What does the attribute of simplicity signify when applied to God? It cannot be an explanatory formula, valid in some way for a transcendent object, for God is in no way similar to an object. On the contrary, the attribute of simplicity acquires meaning if we make it the content of a reductive act. We say that God is simple or that he is superessential, because we can, by reduction, sever the essence-existence (or subject-object) correlation and disengage a spontaneity free from all composition. To "reduce" the multiple, at the intelligible level (which remains one and multiple), and to discover that God is simple [9] are the same thing. The attribute is nothing other than the notion in which the result of a reductive intention is inscribed. It witnesses to the success of the intention; but to understand it, one must himself effect the movement that it summarizes.

9. In short, to affirm that God is simple is to intend him by way of the *one-multiple* through reducing the multiple. Without this reduction, the irreducible could not be attained.

An enumeration of the divine attributes would have only scholarly interest. Our purpose is not to write a treatise of natural theology. It is to outline a critique of the idea of God and its schemes. More important to us than a list of attributes (that can be found in the manuals [10]) is the signification and scope of attribution itself. Now if there are concepts, such as simplicity, unity, and spontaneity, that can be regarded as content of the reductive act, there are others that give pause: infinity, immutability, omnipresence, intelligence, will, freedom, love, life, blessedness. In fact the first three in this group express negations (infinity, immutability), or at least a relation to the finite (omnipresence); they can be truly *reduced* or applied to the Absolute only if transcendence is thought simultaneously with them. Likewise, the last six concepts, plus eternity (a negative aspect of which is presented by immutability), can refer to the intelligible as well as to God. Consequently, rather than ending with these concepts, reduction must set out from them. And when it does so, it always opens onto the trans-ordinal God, in whom the distinctions between intelligence and intelligible, intelligence and will, freedom and necessity, and time and eternity are transcended. The concepts life, blessedness, and even love [11] call for reduction, since language uses them at extremely diverse levels. Consequently, everything happens as if the classical attributes are distributed on different planes. The purest would express the "irreducible"; the others, being inferior to them by one or two degrees,

10. Let us refer to the manual of manuals, the *Summa Theologica*, I.a. Q. 3, 4, 6, 7, 8, 9, 10, 11, 13, etc.

11. The term charity gives rise to equivocations. It connotes immediately the idea of universal grace and, in a Paulinian context, that of descending grace.

postulate successive purifications. To the degree that the same act of reduction traverses the diverse strata of attributes, the latter punctuate the stages of a single movement. In this respect, they are complementary not despite their unequal lack of adequation, but *because* of it. At any rate, the same Absolute is intended by them. It will be said that transcendence is not customarily classed among the attributes.[12] The reason is that this term was not used until rather recently.[13] Everything considered, it is a less ambiguous term than "infinite." Stressing the negation of all spatial reference is, however, less important than exposing the trans-ordinal character that marks the extreme point of reduction and

12. Eastern theology, so sensitive to the idea of transcendence, has a curious but suggestive manner of conceiving the divine attributes. It assimilates them to the "energies" through which the divine essence spontaneously radiates before manifesting itself in the economy of salvation. Vladimir Lossky writes, "One could say, to use a familiar term, that the energies are the attributes of God. However, these dynamic and concrete attributes have nothing in common with the concept-attributes ascribed to God by the abstract and sterile theology of the manuals. . . . God is determined by none of his attributes. All determinations are inferior to Him, and are logically posterior to the essence of his Being in itself." (*La théologie mystique de l'Église d'Orient*, Paris, 1944, pp. 77–78.) [English translation by a small group of members of The Fellowship of St. Alban and St. Sergius, *The Mystical Theology of the Eastern Church* (London, 1957), p. 80.] Lossky assures us that this is why Orthodox thought would not be at home in St. Augustine's trinitarian psychology.

13. According to Lalande (*Vocabulaire technique et critique de la philosophie*, 5th ed., p. 1121), the term *transcendent* appears in many different senses in Pascal, Berkeley, and Kant. We noted earlier that in our time it is opposed to *immanent*, whose contrary in the Middle Ages was *transitive*. We have already indicated that the terms *trans-ascendence* and *trans-descendence* were proposed by Jean Wahl at the December 4, 1937 meeting of the Société Française de Philosophie.

gives the various acts of attribution their true scope.[14] If
God is conceived as trans-ordinal, attribution no longer
has the meaning of a predicative inherence in the
subject God.[15] It is equivalent to a specific intentionality
which, through reduction, discloses the thought and
lived meaning of the relation of the spirit to God.[16]

14. In the classical tradition, the idea of perfection was
regarded as a divine attribute. It has the advantage of bringing to
mind a qualitative maximum, an optimum. On the other hand,
insofar as it evokes the notion of a sum of perfections, it becomes
more confused; it tends to project the constellation of ideas and
values into God, thus compromising the rigor of the attribute of
simplicity.

15. With great precision, Jean Trouillard (cf. *La purification
plotinienne*, Paris, 1955, p. 100) [The French edition incorrectly
refers to Trouillard's *La procession plotinienne*, p. 131.] gives the
reason for the insufficiencies of attribution by inherence. "*All
attribution is addition.* The method, then, is in contradiction with
the goal of the inquiry. The simple being is one who is only
himself in an indistinct intensity. . . . He is attained in himself
and through himself, or he is not attained. Thus our manner of
intending him is the attitude that makes us reject all that we add
to him and to ourselves in order to think him, and since all minds
are 'concentric to God,' it makes us recover the originary point
where we coincide with him." This text is remarkable for the
relationship it establishes between the One and the mind: to
think God is first of all to *think by means of God*, that is, to
employ intelligible mediations that permit the mind to return
toward the One from which it proceeds. Thus conversion and
procession will attempt to coincide. By instituting mediations,
however, one multiplies and adds; by comprehending them, one
concentrates and simplifies. At the limit, when the contemplation
is sufficiently intense, simplicity is intended and unity is
attained. The paradox is confirmed: to rejoin the simple, one
must first of all advance into the multiple, although the latter is
subsequently reduced in order to discover what unifies it at its
root.

16. In a rather different context from ours, Jeanne Hersch
writes the following: "Truth, justice, form—three notions that,
taken in their completeness, in their entirety without residue, in
their purity as Ideas, do not tell man what God is. They do tell
toward what horizon of the spiritual heavens men turn in order
to love God; they tell the meaning of men's adoration and the

When this intentional act has linked, step by step, the different mediations, thanks to which the spirit discovers its dependence on the One, it has accomplished its task. On the one hand, it has regulated and focused the spirit's intention. On the other hand, it has grasped that the intention is due to us and that God escapes all grasping (as such, he is "irreducible"). Thus, a norm of attribution takes shape that, far from reducing God to the sphere of an explanatory logic, preserves his sovereign originality.[17] We can and must call him *transcategorial*, and from now on it will be understood why. God is not less than what the mind is capable of producing in a determinate manner when it progresses toward unity. He can only be more. But to have the right to declare that he is more, one must have effected the primordial acts that permit the subject to "reduce" itself, that is, to disengage what is or is not *absolutely* valuable. It is not sufficient that an intention be valid for

---

direction of their quest. They are pointers, not names." She adds, "terms of prayer, not of description," specifying later that *prayer* designates an intentional efficacy of the living consciousness. Miss Hersch concludes with this summary: "One does not leave the human behind. The spiritual act that transcends the human remains specifically human. It does not express the being of transcendence but the human transcendence of the human." (Cf. *L'Être et la forme*, Neuchâtel, 1946, pp. 105–6.) Nevertheless, if the intentionality is correct, it is efficacious; if it is efficacious, the Absolute is attained by the intention, even if he who intends, along with his mode of consciousness, remains incurably relative and human.

17. "Perhaps the essential thing for man," writes Deschoux, "is to resist the constant temptation to attribute his own limits to God (in the very effort he makes to exempt God from them), and in one manner or another to make himself a God, since he sets himself up as judge and measure of God." (*Initiation à la philosophie*, Paris, 1951, p. 70.) We think we have escaped this fault. However, our refusal to determine God does not culminate, as does that of Deschoux, in a religion of immanence.

some given order; it must be valid beyond even the
notion of order. Otherwise it could not be applied to God.
Now, a review of the human categories shows that each,
at least in ordinary usage, is relative to the others. Their
interdependence proves that none of them is sufficient
by itself. As determinations, which by definition are
reciprocal negations, they compose a system. In these
conditions, we cannot transplant our categories as such
into God; reduction must sift them through the
screen. Yet what we can and must do is to use our
categories in such a fashion as to tighten our thought
still more, until the reductive act is in position to
liberate the irreducible part of each one of them. Or, if
the act succeeds in dissolving one category or another, it
is a sign that the vanquished category is subordinate to
another category that is more resistant and capable of
sustaining the test of criticism.

Thus we succeed in reinstating the trans-categorial
without betraying any of the categories or the Absolute.
The latter would quickly fall back below the spirit if he
were not correctly intended by way of the highest
spiritual exigencies.[18]

18. Gilson wrote the following in 1913: "The creature must be
reminded that between the finite and the infinite, or as Gibieuf
says, the superinfinite that is God, there is an irreducible
difference of nature and that this difference must remain present
to his thought when he wishes to speak properly of his creator.
When one applies the method of analogy to God, he constantly
exposes himself to the danger of anthropomorphism. And for
someone who wants to form a correct idea of divine grace it is
extremely important to divest his conception of the nature of God
of all anthropomorphism." (*La liberté chez Descartes et la
théologie*, p. 197.)

[11] AGNOSTICISM AND ANTHROPOMORPHISM

THUS A SOUND critique of the divine attri-
butes, to the extent that it proves the spirit is connected
to God, refutes agnosticism. God is beyond our categories, but he is not outside our spirituality. This critique
seems, however, to concede something to agnosticism.
We intend and attain God, but cannot say that we
determine him. It is impossible to make God enter into a
domain of exchange and direct communication. But
then is not the God of dialogue inconceivable? Will
religion ever transcend the plane of imagination? Here
we meet with the most formidable objection—so formidable that the philosopher of religion is very near to being so fascinated by it that he speaks of nothing else. In
fact, although here we outline a first response, we
reserve the right to take up this central difficulty
elsewhere.

Let us say, to get things started, that what is taken
for our weak point must become our strong point. No,
we do not know God with his eyes; or if we were assured
of contemplating him by borrowing his perspective, it
would be a mystical vision, much superior to the distinct
exercise of the faculties. It remains for us to know him
through our own more or less limited, more or less
efficacious, resources, and especially by means of the
living intentionality that points toward him. By critically
recovering the meaning and value of our relation to
God—a relation constitutive of our spirituality—we are
certain of in no way falsifying or diminishing the scope
of the acts that lead the spirit toward the Absolute. But
is that not simply to credit ourselves with the intrinsic

exigency for unity which is in us witnessing to the presence of the supreme One? Once having found God, we cannot get *inside him* in order to describe him and to see him as he sees himself. We remain prisoners of our categories, constrained to utilize the multiple for discovering the One. This is why intelligence itself, which implies redoubling and multiplicity, is transcended by the One.[19] But if we remain within our frontiers, if we cannot enter into God, we do know how to come *to him*. The reduction that leads us there is not unknown and it is fully ours *de jure* and *de facto*. For us to know God consists neither in surmounting him nor in objectifying him, but in knowing how to perform certain acts that allow us to intend him without missing him, attain him without deforming him, and think him without inserting him into an "order" of thought. In other words, to know God is to know how the spirit can be restored to its principle when it discovers, without alteration or confusion, *that by which* it becomes spirit. In touching the end the spirit rejoins its source, but to remain autonomous the spirit must distinguish itself once more from its source. Why should it establish itself in a theology of coming to God, and how can it maintain itself there?

19. In this sense, the One is super-consciousness and even super-thought. This is not to say that he is less than consciousness or thought. Indivisible unity is presence to self with no lag. For the One, we must conceive, following Plotinus, a type of self-discernment that is not a discrimination which opposes. (Cf. *Enneads* V, 4, 2; trans. Bréhier, p. 81.) [English translation cited above, pp. 401–2.] It is undeniable that the subject runs a risk by climbing toward unknowability. The danger is overcome critically only if one has experienced ideas and relations. Otherwise, there is still the possibility of illusions that would confuse a mysticism of the sensibility with an ethic of the spirit.

Only a theology of return and a theology of derivation—
both theologies of motion—are possible. They complete
one another; they valorize each other as do conversion
and procession. Nothing can transcend them because
nothing can make itself God. Man must limit himself to
recognizing his dependence. Or rather, he must discern
that God upon whom he depends is not that which limits
him. On the contrary, man is limited only because he
has diverged from God. Thus the relationship to God is a
liberation; it can even be a promise of intimate com-
munion with the simplicity of the One.

Still this passage to the One, or this initial relation,
never determines the One himself. God will not reveal
himself to those who wish to hold him under their
regard. Whereas he does manifest himself in the impulse which pushes the spirit to self-position. If some
comparisons are permissible, God is less in front of us,
even as a horizon that extends beyond us, than in us,
as a unity richer than we can grasp. Or again—a
formula which must be carefully understood—he is an
Absolute of exigency, not the *object of an exigency for
the Absolute*.[20] His presence demands that we contest
everything relative, but it supports no objectification.
Because God witnesses to himself in us, at the level
where procession begins, we must lose all hope of
examining him in himself. He can be intended only with
the aid of the plane in which he inscribes his action,
that is, from a point of view which is not his own. On
the other hand, and as a consequence, there is no better

20. If God is in us as an *Absolute of exigency*, it becomes
clear that it is as difficult to prove him in the order of explanation
as to objectify the principle of objectification, that is, *that by
which* objects are, although not itself an object.

knowledge of God than the methodical deciphering of spiritual experience, since the latter accentuates the repercussion of the divine presence in us. By living and thinking in its order, the spirit can read transcendence even in expressive immanence. Likewise, the incarnated consciousness, if it is faithful to the instructions of reduction, can detect that even sensible expressions are laced with the intelligible. From there, step by step, a liaison with God will be established that is distributed on different planes, but is continuous, hierarchical, and oriented. Religion is perhaps (apart from critical reflection, which is a secondary approach) only a series of expressions, distributed according to the diverse levels of consciousness. Thus the philosopher must, from order to order, reinstate what was transposed, reintegrate what was projected, reunify what was spread out in time and space. To criticize religion is thus to concur in a movement of interiorization. Religion is not thereby dissolved, if it is true that the diversity of planes is imposed on concrete consciousness and cannot be suppressed.[21]

Thus, from now on we are justified in rejecting agnosticism. Unknowing persists where unknowability exists. But the ineffable is no less present; and as ineffable it can be expressed only if it gives rise to an expressing that is below it. The intelligible is precisely this capacity of expressing the inexpressible, a capacity not so much for saying it as for doing what bears witness to its action. How can those who understand, or strive to understand, the spirit as expression of God be reproached with ignoring what the Absolute is for consciousness? Yes, the Absolute is unknowable (he is

21. No more than the astronomical sun cancels out the sensible sun.

beyond knowledge),[22] but he is neither reducible nor eliminable. He marks the spiritual life with his imprint and thus is not unrevealable.[23] He at least manifests

22. Raymond Ruyer's imaginative apology for the God who does not happen to be omniscient merits consideration (cf. "L'Expressivité," *Revue de métaphysique et de morale*, January–June, 1955, nos. 1–2, pp. 71–72). God needs neither to know nor to feel natural expressivity. Each order carries in itself its degree or kind of truth. And to perceive the latter one must be in tune with the former. Now God does not have to lower himself to the level of each order, and in the first place, he cannot do it. By thus obliging him, we do not exalt him, but degrade him. It is time, according to Georges Duhamel's picturesque expression, that certain writers stop plundering God as if they were Englishmen in a colonial empire.

23. In a lecture given at Zurich, November 5, 1951 (cf. *Revue de théologie et de philosophie*, Lausanne, 1951, IV, p. 298), Martin Heidegger writes this: "Man's measure is the manner in which God, remaining unknown, reveals himself. This 'appearance' of God is the measure by which man measures himself. The fact of unveiling is what allows the hidden to be seen. In this unveiling it is not a question of tearing away, but of preserving what is hidden in its 'occultation.' Strange measure! *Not grasping, but actions that correspond to the grasp of this measure*. This measure alone gives the measure of man's nature. Man 'lives' by measuring this space between heaven and earth." (I have used Raymond Savioz's translation and added italics.) [The English here is a translation of Savioz's translation.] The following commentary on this sybilline text could be made from our point of view. There is no grasping of God, but there are approaches that express the profound (and even constitutive) attitude of the spirit toward the Absolute. One does not know God (as an object). But because being situated with relation to him and being spirit are the same thing, all orientation toward him (that is, the manner in which the spirit masters its own experience in order to open itself to him) entails various and complex approaches within the heart of consciousness. In short, the spirit is relation to God; the spiritual life is the concrete "exercise" of this relation; the knowledge of God is reflection on this exercise. Neither agnosticism nor notionalism; only a gnoseology inscribed in spiritual immanence, or again, an ensemble of vectors that simultaneously define the spirit in relation to the One and the meaning the One can have in and for the spirit.

himself through signs,[24] and first and foremost through the eminent sign that is the power to signify: the spirit. Next, he manifests himself through things themselves, inasmuch as the spirit makes the world a universe, that is, an ensemble of connected significations.[25] If, then, the Absolute does not speak, the spirit and the world, taken charge of by the spirit, can speak to us of him and for him. How, on any hypothesis, could God speak without taking for an organ the voice of the spirit which echoes in all of creation? But it is not a matter of a simple occasional message, of an episodic intervention, or even of a decisive but contingent call that could brusquely change the destiny of spiritual immanence. It concerns, more profoundly, a permanent contact between God and the spirit, a relationship constitutive of what we are, an intrinsic rapport that permits the spirit to make itself, and in doing so, to manifest God whose image it is. A relationship of this kind cannot, moreover, be exhausted in the unfolding of intelligible operations. It is inevitably reflected even on inferior planes, each one of which possesses a unique economy. From that comes the extreme complexity of the attitude of consciousness toward God; we will devote other works to the analysis of these attitudes. So it was useful to suggest that all revelation of God necessarily passes through the different strata of spiritual immanence.[26]

Specified in detail, our position should now seem

24. As St. Paul says. Through *ciphers,* as Jaspers says. Cf. Mikel Dufrenne and Paul Ricoeur, *Karl Jaspers et la philosophie de l'existence* (Paris, 1947), pp. 286 ff.

25. It is known that St. Bonaventure, following the Victorines, places the spirit, *image* of God, above things, divine *vestiges.* Cf. *Itinerarium mentis in Deum,* chaps. II and III. [Cf. the previous references to translations of this work.]

26. This is why our analysis will borrow the classical approaches of psychology and history.

more clear to the reader. We do not seek in any way to conceal its foundation. For us the trans-ordinal God remains beyond all determination. Consequently, there are neither values nor particular ideas in his essence; they are at the intelligible level, not the level of the One.[27] In strict terms, the Absolute is not conscious, but supra-conscious. Nor is he intelligible; he is super-intelligible. On its side, the spirit, by reason of the tie that unites it to God, is truly *intention of God, dynamic image of him toward him.* This living relationship removes all danger of agnosticism. It manifests the God who is hidden within it; it offers itself as the vehicle of all revelation. If this seems to be a paradox, at least it is justified and fruitful. We do not have to soften the paradox since the context in which it is inscribed anticipates errors of reading. The trans-categorial God is

27. Gilson writes, "By the mere fact of his existence and the superabundance of his essence and goodness, God acts in the way the rich let their treasures fall. He does not act with his eyes fixed on an end and does not pursue a goal that is external to him. It is, on the contrary, the creatures that go out from him, as from their principle, who necessarily tend to return toward him as toward their end." (*La liberté chez Descartes et la théologie,* p. 192.) This shows clearly that finalism is one of our modes of representation and not a system of values pre-posed in God. More clearly still, in summarizing Pseudo-Dionysius and explaining how he subordinates ideas and being to God, Gilson writes, "The ideas, then, represent divine rays, which are scarcely removed from their center, but are, however, already distinguished from it, since they are like the second revelation of the unity within number. The important thing to retain here is that God produces being as his first participation. Thus being is dependent on God, but God is not dependent on being." (*La philosophie au moyen âge,* 2nd ed., Paris, 1944, p. 84.) [A parallel but not identical passage will be found in Gilson's *History of Christian Philosophy in the Middle Ages* (New York, 1955), p. 84.] With Pseudo-Dionysius (who follows Plotinus), we situate the ideas and being below God, but we emphasize that God, in order to pose ideas and values, must first of all permit the spirit to pose itself.

never a stranger to us, because he renders spiritual
immanence expressive—and it in turn renders the
sensible order expressive. If, nevertheless, this expressivity of immanence does not throw us back to immanentism, it is because reduction is capable of deciphering it. This implies the simultaneous discovery of the
inward orientation of the spirit and the trans-ordinal
character of the Absolute. In other words, there is no
danger of making the One slide into the intelligible
plane, even when the latter alone has the capacity to
proclaim and witness that God is its source. God cannot
be confounded with the intelligible order, or vice versa,
because God is not an order. They will never occupy the
same plane. Neither pantheism nor immanentism is to
be feared. And with greater reason, there is no danger of
psychologism, mobilism, etc., because the intelligible
transcends the empirical and God transcends the intelligible.[28]

[III] THE ABSOLUTE OF DIALOGUE
AND THE ABSOLUTE OF EXIGENCY

RECALLING THESE distinctions sets the gross-
est confusions aside. It remains to examine two previously mentioned difficulties: that of an *Absolute of
dialogue*, and that of the assistance that God gives to the
spirit.

28. When God is called Word or Logos, it is not insinuated
that like consciousness he suffers the subject-object division, for
his act does not admit of falling back. Thus the conception of a
divine Word is not opposed to the One's transcendence to the
intelligible. We make this better understood in our *Philosophie de
la religion* by recovering the true meaning of the trinitarian
speculations.

It is well known how much the religious consciousness seems attached to an Absolute of dialogue. By
criticizing the latter do we not irremediably compromise
the religious exchange between God and man? No; the
most that can be said is that criticism withdraws this
exchange from psychological and sociological metaphors
in order to situate it on a more profound plane. The
dialogue no longer goes from the *ego* to the divine *alter
ego* (that representation would be a distortion). It goes
from spiritual singularity to God's productive simplicity
which creates the spirit as self-creator.[29] Thus there is
purification and interiorization. This is a valuable gain
and an increase in rigor that preserves the essence of
religion and protects it from the reproaches that an
excessively anthropomorphic piety merits.[30] Still, by

29. The thesis of self-creation is taken up in detail in our
Philosophie de la religion, Part One.

30. Psychological piety readily takes God as a conscience-
witness. We have shown the danger of this in taking account of
certain of J. P. Sartre's criticisms (cf. *Foi et interrogation,* p.
118). The God-witness is like a double of the personal conscience;
it is its judge (this provokes fear) and also its refuge (this evokes
confidence and abandon). The God of justice thus becomes, and
without inconsistency, the God of mercy. However, if this
ambivalence is not transcended, the Absolute, according to the
criticism of Nietzsche (and some contemporaries), remains a God
of weakness who distributes the premiums of security and offers
celestial eternity as an alibi for terrestrial engagement. After our
critical purifications, taking into account above all that for us the
Absolute is the power of the exigency for the Absolute rather than
the object of this exigency, God no longer appears as the
complement of our deficiencies, but as the spring of our energy.
Religion, rightly understood, is content neither with the consolations of God nor with the God of consolations. It is not enough for
God to be the force of our weakness; he must be the force of our
force. Rilke writes, "In order to find God, it is necessary to be
happy, because those who invent him through distress move too
quickly and explore too little the intimacy of his burning
absence." (Cited in *Deucalion,* 4, p. 156.)

means of a dangerous symmetry, there will be a tendency to place at the margin of this thesis an impersonal Absolute, as indifferent as it is immovable. Is it not impersonal if it cannot enter into a person to person dialogue? Is it not indifferent if ideas and values are brought into play below it? It must be answered that a God-Reason, an axiomatic Absolute, perhaps would be impersonal and indifferent. A trans-ordinal God can only be the contrary, since all limiting attributes are thrust far from him. If, as we believe, the spirit personalizes or singularizes itself at the intelligible plane, the One, from which it proceeds, cannot be infra-personal, but rather is trans-personal. The clumsy epithet "impersonal" does not recognize that the One is more than person rather than less.[31] As for indifference, it must be said that there is indeed an apathy of sensibility and judgment in God.[32] But only the notion of creation or procession sufficiently accentuates the generosity of God. He poses the constitutive relation of the spirit;[33] thus it is through the most intimate interior,

31. Lachelier (cf. *Oeuvres*, II, Paris, 1933, p. 161) is especially careful not to make God support the restrictions of the personal life (intelligence united to a sensibility). Nevertheless, he admits that if care is taken to make the necessary purifications, God can be called "absolute personality." (*Ibid.*, I, p. 14.)

32. A contrary conception of God would oblige one to speak, with Proclus and Pseudo-Dionysius, of *anthropopathism*. Cf. H. Koch, *Pseudo-Dionysius in seinen Beziehungen zum Neuplatonismus und Mysterienwesen Philologus* (Mainz, 1900), pp. 198 and 260.

33. Brunschvicg's eloquent text is well known. "That there is between God and man no other relation than that of spirit to spirit, such as the doctrine of the inner Word expresses, has remained a paradox and a scandal in the history of Western thought; for it is as if man must therefore attribute the divine nature to himself. But man does not stop knowing that he is minute in the ponderous mass of the universe when he counts the stars by tens of thousands, and ephemeral in the temporal

through the influx of the processive motion, that God is found to be in contact with spiritual persons. One could not conceive a more profound "philanthropy" on the part of God. But the terminology of dialogue, even if it

sequence when he projects the reality of a nebula to the distance of some tens of millions of light years. On the other hand, God would cease to be God if we lacked courage and subordinated spiritual presence to the conditions of space and time. And undoubtedly, a God having a point of contact with no privileged determination of extension or duration, a God who neither takes initiative nor assumes responsibility in the physical aspect of the universe, who wills neither the ice of the poles nor the heat of the tropics, who is sensitive to neither the grandeur of the elephant nor the minuteness of the ant, neither the harmful action of a microbe nor the helpful effect of a pill, a God who does not intend to accuse us of our sins or those of our ancestors, who does not know more unfaithful men than rebellious angels, who fulfills neither the prediction of the prophet nor the miracle of the magician, a God who dwells neither in the sky nor on the earth, who is apprehended at no particular moment of history, who speaks no language and is translated into none, is a God who, from the point of view of a primitive mentality or the 'gross supernaturalism' that William James advocated so clearly, would be called an 'abstract ideal.'" (*La Progrès de la conscience*, II, pp. 796–97.) Eloquence here has piled up too many negations from diverse orders, but Brunschvicg's thought can be grasped: God is not responsible for the material world; he cannot be tied to it. If Brunschvicg would content himself with making a critique of the idea of contingency, if he would distinguish between the relation of the spirit to God and that of God to the world, if the God he speaks of were not measured by the dimensions of the intelligible order (which, for him, are on the same plane with rational constructions), his denials could pass for critical purifications and not simple negations. It has been seen that like Brunschvicg we reject *descending creation* (in the sense of a dialectic of being) and are sympathetic to the notion of *ascending creation;* but we safeguard *procession* (a dialectic from the One, very different from causal ontology). This is why, in our sense, God is manifested in derived terms, not first of all by contingent and extrinsic expressions, but through the processive motion itself. Thus the intelligible bears witness to him at the heart of self-position. The sensible, according to us, attests him only mediately, because it proceeds from the intelligible and is more within the range of incarnated consciousness, gives only a feeble translation of it.[34]

Nevertheless—and this is the second point we have to elucidate—the dialogic exchange seems to be a more direct reciprocity, i.e., face to face. Whereas an Absolute, whose contribution is to render possible the spirit's self-position, seems elusive even in its manner of being present. In fact, does not this presence of the back side rather than the face, of propulsion without predetermination, and of exigency without pledged assurance, resemble an enigmatic force that carries us toward the unknown, and perhaps intrigue? Certainly an Absolute that pushes us to search with lamentation is worth more than Absolutes of facility and resignation. Yet is there not something other here than a tribute to the immanent source that always gives us the movement to go further? In short, can we be content with an Absolute that throws us into becoming, that provokes us to the pursuit of an inaccessible good? Brunschvicg's cult of unity immediately comes to mind. "God will not be born from an externally directed intention such as that which places us in the presence of a thing or person. It is precisely God for whom existence will not be different from essence. And this essence will be manifested only from within, thanks to the reflective effort that discovers, in

---

is its projection. Thus we would repudiate the physical creationism that Brunschvicg challenges, without introducing his dualism that makes the spirit a stranger in the world and God the means by which the spirit calls itself absolute.

34. In fact, the body of religion, its historical expression, is enunciated in this terminology of dialogue, covenant, etc. It goes without saying that the religious soul, in raising itself to spiritual reciprocity, turns this vocabulary inside out and transcends it. The category of dialogue thus mediates an intention that transcends the plane on which the relations between God and consciousness are expressed in psycho-sociological terms.

the indefinite progress of which our thought is capable, the eternity of intelligence and the universality of love. We do not doubt that God exists, since we always feel ourselves, in Malebranche's words, impelled to go further, even to the luminous sphere that appears at the summit of the Platonic dialectic where, above the being's imagination, the unity of the One is sufficient and answers for itself. To meditate on unity brings us there." [35] This beautiful text harmonizes at several points with theses we defend; nevertheless, it diverges from our thought. Besides confounding the One with the intelligible, it understands unity only as the acceleration of an unlimited movement. Eternity is conceived simply as the generator of progress—moreover, a progress that admits of regression since few consciousnesses elevate themselves to unity and even fewer maintain themselves there. This is why the ages of intelligence have highs and disconcerting lows. A system of criticized mobilism is no less a mobilism. An indefinite quest is interesting in that it refers to an inexhaustible good, but is discouraging since it is always for tomorrow and not today. We believe, on the contrary, that the indefinite is thinkable only by means of the infinite, a living infinite that is present to the spirit at each moment. The finite can repeat itself indefinitely only as expression of the infinite.[36] Without the perpetual motion of absolute spontaneity, without the permanent liaison of the spirit to God, no order, either intelligible or sensible, can

35. *Héritage de mots, héritage d'idées*, p. 57.
36. Let us recall here Boutroux's happy formula, "The finite can imitate the infinite only by diversifying itself infinitely." (*Science et religion dans la philosophie contemporaine*, new ed., Paris, 1947, p. 392.) [English translation by Jonathon Nield, *Science and Religion in Contemporary Philosophy* (London, 1909), p. 399.]

possibly unfold.[37] The slightest effective initiative and
the least reflective act pass at each instant through this
hidden center from whence surges the originary spark
that, at our level, bursts into light and love, thought and
will. Yes, we do always have the impulse to go further.
We have it because that which returns to the source
coincides with what comes from the source; consequently, to return is to set out again, and to conclude is
to embark. The principle that catches us throws us back
again. At least, we touch unity, we use it; it is ours
without being us, in an eternal present that recapitulates the past, continues to make it live, and opens it
onto the future.[38]

37. For the trans-ordinal One can create "orders" only
through the mediation of the *one-multiple*, the intelligible.
Without this distinction one is driven to the contradictions of an
infinite-finite God, dear to certain American philosophers. Cf.
Charles Hartshorne, "La Philosophie de la religion aux États-
Unis," *Les Études philosophiques*, new series, 7th year, nos. 1–2,
1952, pp. 50–56.

38. According to Th. Ruyssen, the notion of transcendence
arises from the call that the future perpetually issues to the
spirit's creative initiative (article cited above, *Revue philosophique*, 1951, p. 529); psychologically, it is explained by the dualism
of actual and potential consciousness (*ibid.*, p. 529). This is to
forget a capital point: if human consciousness has the power to
assure the liaison between past, present, and future, it is because
it borrows it from pure unity, absolute spontaneity. Not unified,
we circulate, as Blondel repeated, among our disjointed elements
(thought, being, action). This proves that we imply the Unity
beyond all determination. In addition, the experience of transcendence (if we can use that expression) is given less by our
openness onto the future than by our *present* power to challenge
and jeopardize any determinate value. Certain authors believe
that this contestation is sufficiently explained through human
freedom. That is debatable since, as we have shown, the
reduction obliges the I to recognize itself as *one and multiple* and
to disclose, apart from any confusion with it, the supreme One. In
this sense, it can be said that to exercise the power of putting
everything in question, including oneself, is, if not to experience
God, at least to really employ him.

Thus the incoherence of an eternity that hemorrhages into time is avoided. Even an Absolute of exigency, in contrast to the exigency for an absolute-object, never submits us to a dialectic of pure *fieri*. Only an obscure and unconscious force would accommodate itself to a becoming without breaks or limits. But the God who transcends all order remains the source of the intelligible order where laws are eternal, where each freedom imposes norms on itself in order to be able to pose itself. Consequently, the Absolute can indeed maintain itself above ideas and values, be more than a person, more than a consciousness, in a word, be a simple unity which we can neither dominate nor objectify. He is preserved as well from gross confusions with natural or biological force. Even more, the Absolute does not allow himself to be trapped by his role as the driving force of the indefinite progress. Trans-ordinal, he does not have to descend in order to animate the orders. His spontaneity can render them productive in their turn, without being placed at their level, without being enclosed in their finitude. On the contrary, it is by remaining in his sovereign unity that the Absolute can promote, within and through the spirit, a unification of the multiple.[39] Thus it is proper to name the Absolute both immanent and transcendent. He is present at the

39. To this argument, we can join another that will show why God, Absolute of exigency, is not reduced to the impulsion of becoming (Brunschvicg). The *exigency* must be judged by its quality, not by the indefinitely extendable number of its applications. In us, the exigency for the Absolute, from the beginning, transcends and makes irreal all the relative. And certainly it is because each relative deceives us that we go from object to object, as Don Juan goes from conquest to conquest. Thus becoming reappears, but as a consequence. The exigency is always taken from another order; or more exactly, it expresses, at our level, the continually actual presence of the principle that dominates all the orders.

heart of the spirit, yet not enclosed there. Present and absent, manifest and hidden, acting but sufficient to himself, the One is indeed that which moves us. But he is first of all, essentially, the pure energy that surges and overflows by himself. As such he is worthy of being called *Absolute,* that which is released from all attachment and disengaged from all determination.

Conclusion

IN OTHER WORKS [1] we will have occasion to return to the problem of God. Here we have only specified the essentials; the detailed consequences will be presented elsewhere. To close the present series of inquiries it is sufficient to recall our goal and systematically assemble the results obtained.

Our intention was to submit to rational criticism the idea of God and its principal scheme, transcendence.[2] To do that we drew this idea from the heart of religion and, more precisely, from Christianity which in the West has raised it to an unequaled height. Then we tried to submit it to philosophical treatment. This proved to be possible only on a double condition: 1) that religion consents not to evade criticism; 2) that philosophy

1. Cf. *Philosophie de la religion*, I–II.
2. It could be said that "transcendence" is a concept, or a category, like "absolute" (whose etymology also betrays a spatial reference). We prefer to regard it as a scheme associated with the idea of God, because it symbolizes what intending God effects or contains. Better, it sustains this intention in order to permit it to detach itself from the "orders" it utilizes and passes through.

[127]

agrees to play its true role of not supplanting living spirituality, but seeking to comprehend it, to specify its diverse activities, and to judge its orientation. When these two conditions are fulfilled, faith and reason render mutual service without excluding one another or combining.

This approach has yielded the following results.

1) It is impossible to make the idea of God enter an objective and homogeneous series of categories that is applicable to derived beings. Any objectivist logic will fail when applied to the Absolute.

2) It is necessary to appeal to *reduction* to take account of the manner in which spontaneous thought leads to God. Reduction is neither mechanical reasoning nor triumphant intuition; at its summit, it is the simultaneous discovery that the multiple is dependent and that the One is present. But this discovery is less an entrance into the evidence than a militant conversion which implies detachment from everything and from self.

3) We disclosed the trans-ordinal and trans-categorial character of God. That is, God is not discovered as an order of truth or superior reality. He is discovered as pure unity, as radical spontaneity, as *that by which* the diverse orders, and even the notion of order, are conceivable.

4) There is a clear opposition between ontology and henology, or metaphysics of Being and metaphysics of the One. The first is able to preserve the sovereignty of God only through added correctives, while the second can do it by virtue of an internal exigency.

5) We purified the scheme of transcendence and defended its spiritual sense, which refers to the simplicity of the One.

6) The divine attributes are to be defined as intentional acts or reductive intentions, not as predicative and descriptive terms.

7) The expression, *the Absolute of dialogue*, which religion seems to authorize or require, is ambiguous. Thus it is necessary to purge all anthropomorphism from the relation of the spirit to God. Consequently, it is necessary to show that the dialogue between God and man is a mode of representation, relative to certain planes of consciousness. The spirit bears the expenses of this transaction, although the Absolute, who sustains and attracts the spirit, authenticates its activities and representations, even the inferior ones, since they cooperate in the victorious return toward the One.

8) The authentic Absolute, the power of an unlimited progress, must be distinguished from an impersonal principle. We presented the Absolute of exigency as an ever actual presence, constantly moving because continually creative.

These results, if free from error, seem to be a real gain for the philosophy of religion. Without the philosophy of religion, the facticious antithesis of the God of philosophers and the God of tradition would continue to hold sway; the roles of criticism and spiritual life would be badly assigned; finally, on the subject of God, the philosopher would prove too much or too little,[3] and

3. Too little, if he is content with a God in harmony with sensible, vital, or psychological evidence; too much, if he presumes to found the transcendence of God on objective supports. The gods of nature, life, and empirical consciousness are false gods. The true God is found only through the mediation of the intelligible, which tears the subject away from psychological egocentricity. Still, it is necessary to know how to go beyond the intelligible and renounce every explanatory doctrine of God.

religion would be ignorant of what, critically, justifies or threatens it. Already, by showing the ambiguity of an Absolute of dialogue and then justifying that function,[4] we furnished an example of the utility of the philosophy of religion. Other examples could be given. Even if the reader does not ratify all the points we have advanced, he must at least, it seems, acknowledge that criticism rigorously purifies the idea of God. It shelters it from psycho-sociological deformations; it does not reduce it to a mysterious X that would be of no value for man. Certainly a relapse is possible in every case. The Absolute, once restored to his true dignity, can be disfigured again. But the demotion itself never annuls the promotion. The idea, lost, recovered, and lost again, will remain active even under the error that masks it. So it is sufficient for us to have established that the Absolute allows himself to be neither eliminated nor circumscribed by consciousness. Man fails to deny or to capture him; he cannot grasp him as an object, but the Absolute does not permit man to lose contact. This is the defeat of sacrilege and agnosticism. Respect for mystery and dependence on mystery go together. For man, it is a matter of recognizing this dependence and conserving this respect, a double duty that obliges him not to be content with a God cut to his size.[5] Man must abandon

4. We will have to do it in a more complete fashion by criticizing the details of the religious evidence. Cf. *Philosophie de la religion*.

5. André Malraux writes, "Fifty years ago psychology reintegrated the demons into man. That is the real importance of psychoanalysis. I think that the task of the next century, in face of the most terrible menace humanity has known, will be to reintegrate the gods." ("L'Homme et le fantôme," *L'Express*, no. 104, May 21, 1955, p. 15.) This reintegration of the divine into the human began, in reality, with philosophy itself. If it consists in a return to spiritual interiority, it can be an homage to the

anthropomorphism, even if it is impossible—no one sees God without dying—to escape *theandrism*.

---

true God. If it limits itself to discovering the Absolute as a dimension of man, it will, after the fashion of the anonymous philosopher mentioned earlier, do too much or too little. Too much, because God is the Ineffable; he is neither our speech, nor our making, nor our action. Too little, for admitting a presence of God to the spirit goes further than self-knowledge; it leads consciousness toward a renewal of perspectives that contrasts clearly with cultural, philanthropic, or technological humanisms.

Index of Names